War Eagle:
Melanie Oakes Harrison
Harriet Oakes Deason

Ain't No Easy Way in Life, Baby!

a tale of two sisters

by

Harriet Oakes Deason
and
Melanie Oakes Harrison

Contents

Foreword

This story is dedicated to the Auburn Tigers of 2013 who worked so hard to change the way they were perceived by others and by themselves. The players, with the help and guidance of their coaches became a Team of Destiny by developing a game plan, perfecting that plan and executing the plan as a team. A lot of prayers and a few miracles along the way also enhanced their success.

The story is also dedicated to Coach Pat Dye whose post-game speech to his Auburn team after they defeated Alabama in 1989 was an inspiration to Melanie and Harriet. Coach Dye was instrumental in bringing the Iron Bowl to Auburn where it had always belonged. After the historic Iron Bowl game in 1989, Coach Dye said the crowd responded to the victory like people who had been liberated from military occupation. He also told his players in the locker room after the game about how their hard work and dedication had paid off and ultimately nothing worth having or accomplishing comes without sacrifice and hard work. He said, "This is the reason we work you in the summertime, and January and February and the Spring.....Ain't no easy way in life."

So, our hats off to the Auburn Tigers of 2013 and to all of the Auburn Tigers who went before them. They all tried, they worked hard, and they all wanted to win. And, thanks to Coach Dye whose forward thinking and steadfastness moved Auburn toward a prominent position among other nationally recognized football programs.

And, thank you, Gus, for a magical, wonderful, fabulous, phenomenal and thrilling season. We love you, Gus. You are smarter than the average bear.

Introduction

More than 95,000 spectators made their way to the Rose
Bowl on January 6, 2014, to cheer their respective teams,
the Tigers and the Seminoles, to victory. Most of them
probably had uneventful journeys to the west coast from all
over the world. That was not the case for the Team of
Destiny II, Melanie Oakes Harrison and Harriet Oakes
Deason. But, then, why would it have been uneventful,
because as Coach Dye so eloquently stated in 1989 after
Auburn defeated Alabama, "Ain't no easy way in life".
And, just as Auburn's defeat of Alabama in 1989 was a
momentous event in Auburn history and a feat that will
forever be remembered, the journey to California was
equally unforgettable and momentous for the two old girls
from Sprott, Alabama.

The journey actually began on November 23, 1963, the day
after President John F. Kennedy was assassinated. Melanie
and Harriet, along with their parents, Norma and Harold
Oakes, and their maternal grandparents, Faye and Norman
Miller, attended their first Auburn football game. The
Auburn Tigers, who at that time were sometimes referred to
as "The Plainsmen", played against the Florida State
Seminoles that day and won. John McAfee, their cousin,
was a defensive tackle on Auburn's team; a team that was
so awesome it was dubbed "The Avalanche". After the
girls met each member of the team on that day in 1963 and
carried home an autographed game day program, Elvis
Presley and The Beatles paled by comparison. Those
handsome young men of the Auburn football team forever
became rock stars for the "the purdy girls from Sprott" a
term their cousin coined as he greeted them one day in
Sewell Hall. The two girls spent many hours leafing
through the autographed game day program just trying to
decide which young man was really the most beautiful.

Tucker Frederickson always got ranked in first place with Bill Cody and Jimmy Sidle tying for second, while George Rose was always among the top contenders for high ranking. At the game, the fans cheered wildly as George awaited a kick at the goal line and they screamed, "All the way, Rose Baby, all the way!" And so for 50 years, Auburn has been the dream team of the two sisters from Sprott. The fact that Harriet's son, Larkin, many years later, lettered in football at Auburn only added to the fervor with which they supported their team.

There was never a hesitation in the spring of 2013 when the order blank for season tickets arrived. There was no doubt about whether the sisters would go to see their Auburn Tigers play one more year. The memories of sitting in the stadium during the previous season to watch Auburn lose one game after another, and then lose to the new kids on the block from A&M, and how they had stayed there through each game, ever hopeful, until the last second ticked off the clock, were somehow fading and not so painful. And, oh my, how the season in 2013 turned out to be the most incomprehensible turn-around in all of sports history.

The year got off to a rocky start with little confidence that the 2013 team was any better than the 2012 team. But, everyone soon began to "get on the Gus Bus". Week by week, hope grew stronger that it might be possible to beat Alabama. Harriet wore her "Beat Alabama" pin to every game she attended, except the Tennessee game. Her brother-in-law, Frank, an Alabama fan, attended that game with Melanie, Harriet, and her husband Cleve, so out of deference to his ability to put up with them and attend an Auburn game, she did not wear the pin. No one ever guessed they should also believe that Auburn would win the SEC Championship and because of a convoluted sequence of losses by other teams and Auburn victories, Auburn would become the team that would travel to the Rose Bowl to play for the BCS National Championship.

As the season evolved, posters began to appear in the stands in growing numbers with the slogans, "In Gus We Trust" and "Don't Mess with the Vest". A buzz could be felt in growing intensity at each game that electrified the stadium and soon the Auburn fans were cheering wildly for a team that only a year before had given them nothing at all to cheer about.

The path that Auburn followed to reach the pinnacle of college football is by now almost legendary----sacking Johnny Football in the last seconds of the game to secure a win over A&M (Thank you, Dee Ford!), the "Miracle in Jordan Hare" to defeat a Georgia team that just wouldn't quit (Thank you, Nick Marshall and Ricardo Louis!), the "kick six" to beat Alabama, with yes, only one second left on the clock (Thank you, Nick Saban and Chris Davis!), Ohio State's defeat on that fateful evening of December 7 at the hands of Michigan State sealed the deal (Thank you, Jesus!) and Auburn was on the way to California!

Shortly after the BCS bowl bids were announced on Sunday night, Melanie called Harriet and asked, "Do you want to go?" Going to the Rose Bowl had really not occurred to Harriet and although she did WANT to go, she hadn't really planned to go to the game. So, after a short discussion, the subject of attending the game was dropped. The next morning, Melanie sent an email to Harriet to let her know that she had "come to her senses" and had decided not to go to the game.

On December 22, Cleve, Harriet and their daughter Courtney, went to "take Christmas" with Melanie and

Frank at their home on the Alabama River in Autaugaville. While Courtney, Melanie and Harriet were sitting around visiting with each other before dinner, Melanie looked at Harriet and said, "Don't you want to go?" Harriet, sensing that Melanie was really serious about going to the game, asked Melanie how much she thought the trip would cost. So, Melanie went over the details of several different scenarios that some of her friends had discussed. After weighing the options, they decided that night, sitting in Melanie's kitchen, that they were LA bound. They rationalized that they were old and might never have the opportunity to go to watch Auburn play in a championship game again and they had always wanted to see the Rose Bowl. Melanie became the appointed agent to make the travel arrangements for the trip, which she did swiftly and with great expertise. And so it was that the trip was planned and the two sisters would soon be on their way to the BCS National Championship Game.

There were many conversations between the two about what they would wear, what they would do, when they would leave, and how they would transport food and drinks on the bus ride between Las Vegas and Los Angeles. The plan was to fly from Birmingham to Las Vegas by way of Charlotte and Dallas on Sunday, January 5, then ride a charter bus from Las Vegas to the Rose Bowl on Monday and then back to Las Vegas after the game Monday night. Then after a day in Las Vegas, they would fly out of Las Vegas Tuesday night and after stops in Los Angeles and Charlotte, would arrive back in Birmingham on Wednesday morning around 10:00 a.m.

The two sisters worked diligently to overcome their ingrained habit of packing most of their earthly belongings to carry with them on the trip. They strategized that with all of the plane and airline changes they were facing on their journey it would be best to travel light and not check luggage. As it turned out, that was one of the smartest decisions they made. When they departed for their trip, each of them had two carry-on bags and tucked inside of one of Melanie's bags was a cooler folded neatly in the bottom. That cooler would be unfolded once they arrived in Las Vegas and used to pack food and beverages for their bus ride from Las Vegas to Pasadena.

Just before it was time for Harriet to leave Sprott, Courtney surprised her with a wonderful travel gift for both she and Melanie. It was a large, white gift bag decorated by Courtney especially for the trip. It reminded Courtney of the lunch bags that her mother decorated when she and Larkin went on class field trips while they were in elementary school. And inside this big white bag, were such wonderful goodies; Snickers, Heath Bars and chocolate footballs stuffed into orange and white polka dot bags, a roll of toilet tissue to use at the end of the game to roll the palm trees at the Rose Bowl, an Auburn compact, lotion in bottles decorated with Auburn logos, an undetermined number of miniature bottles full of Red Stag, Maker's Mark, and Crown Royal, and last but not least, 2 cigarettes attached to the bag with shiny blue ribbons for a "victory smoke".

The artwork on the bag cleverly depicted the two sisters on board an airplane on their way to California. It also had a magnificent sketch of the Rose Bowl, replete with palm trees out front that were bedecked with tiny strips of toilet paper, and of course, the words from Pat Dye's 1989 speech that had become the two sisters' bylines during the 2013 season---"Ain't no easy way in life, BABY!", "I ain't smart enough to tell you how I feel about you", and "This is why we work hard in the Spring." Across the top of the bag was a musical score parodying Jan and Dean's lyrics, "the little old ladies to Pasadena."

Go Granny, Go Granny, Go Granny, Go!!!

Birmingham

Cleve and Harriet met Melanie in Pelham for lunch that Sunday. Cleve was insistent that they must get to the airport early. They left his truck and Melanie's car at Cleve's workplace, Warrior Tractor in Pelham, Alabama, and drove in the Flex to the airport. The plan was for Cleve to take the Flex back to Pelham after he delivered the pair to the airport and leave it with Melanie's car safely locked inside the fenced yard at Warrior Tractor to avoid paying airport parking fees. They reasoned that money that wasn't used to pay parking fees would increase the amount of money they would have to spend for souvenirs and the slot machines in Las Vegas. So, Cleve drove them to the airport and after several enthusiastic hugs and kisses the sisters were off on their journey to California.

Melanie, being the expert air traveler, was able to provide instructions to Harriet about making her way through security and having everything in order. But before going through security, they decided to have something to drink to ease them into their long flight. They mixed a drink with two of the miniatures Courtney had provided for them and a soft drink they bought from the vending machine at the airport, and then sat down in the ticketing area to relax for a few minutes to drink it. They thought it was cool that the vending machine accepted credit cards.

Due to the frigid weather that was descending upon much of the United States, many airports in the northern cities had already begun cancelling flights and shutting down the airports due to ice and snow. Melanie and Harriet thought that their flight would be ok since it originated in Orlando and they would be flying from Birmingham to Charlotte. Melanie had checked and the airport in Charlotte was not experiencing weather-related problems. The news crew from TV 33/40 was at the airport hoping to catch glimpses of and get interviews with woebegone travelers who had not made connections due to the weather conditions or had some pitiful story to tell.

As always, Harriet somehow attracted people who desired small, trivial discussions or favors. Was the word "SUCKER" actually tattooed on her forehead, or was there something in her face that caused people to incorrectly believe that she wanted to be helpful and attentive to every Tom, Dick and Harry in need of a favor? There was the time when a young man approached Harriet in an antiques store and told her about all of his anger and pent up frustrations toward Osama bin Laden and she quietly listened and nodded her head. But, when he got to the finale of his discourse and stated that he had "a *bandana* against bin Laden", she wanted to ask if it was red or blue, but thought better of that idea and simply said, "Me, too", then she left the store. What caused these interactions to occur? Melanie said that it was her "open expression" that caused people to believe that she wanted to be helpful or listen to their stories. So with her "open expression" Harriet was asked if she would babysit the news crew's camera tripod while they traipsed through the airport looking for the forlorn and woebegone newsworthy travelers. When they returned, Melanie and Harriet began to chat with them and found out that the woman was the daughter of Gusty Yearout, former great Auburn football star. They also learned that Jameis Winston's parents and little brother were checking in for a flight to Los Angeles. Gusty's daughter and the sidekick cameraman soon decided that there was nothing tragic enough to report about at the airport, so they left. Later Harriet learned from a co-worker and a childhood friend that she actually appeared on the news that night on a Birmingham station. They didn't say, but she hoped that it was a good shot of her.

Getting through security went off without a hitch; Harriet did not even have to remove her shoes because she and Melanie had somehow attained the status of "special customers". Melanie surmised it was because the reservations had been charged to her credit card and she had been elevated to a special status because of air miles she had logged on business trips. Melanie later learned on another flight that this was actually partially true. She had become a "trusted" individual in the eyes of the TSA and could go through shorter and less stringent security lines. After waiting a short while, the attendant called for passengers to begin boarding. Everyone got all situated in their seats on the plane and then it taxied out onto the runway and prepared to take off. And there they sat, and sat, and sat for what seemed to be an eternity. Then a crackling of the microphone let them know that news was about to come over the speaker and it was not going to be good news. The muffled voice of the pilot over the PA system sounded like an ancient old man. He let them know that the flight was being delayed for a short while, about 15 minutes. Then much later, another announcement from the pilot informed the passengers that the plane would be taxiing back to the terminal where all passengers would deplane. Inclement weather in Charlotte had resulted in an unacceptably low level of visibility and the flight would be delayed because it would not be possible to land there until 11:00 p.m.

They were FOGGED OUT of Charlotte! How could this happen? What was going on in Charlotte? It wasn't even snowing there! Melanie and Harriet wondered if the Charlotte airport and/or the plane they were on did not have radar equipment. Had no one ever heard of an instrument controlled landing? Does that really only happen in the movies? John Wayne or Glen Ford could have gotten them there without a problem and had a little fling with a glamorous woman in the cockpit while landing the plane. The world has gone to Hell in a handbasket since we lost the two of them. A man walked on the moon and a vehicle roved over the surface of Mars, but yet, a plane cannot land in Charlotte just because of a little fog? There is a paradox here that should be examined. But as cousin Jane Harrison would say, "It is what it is!" So now, how were the two sisters going to make the connections in Dallas that would take them to Las Vegas?

Do you suppose the lunar landing module might be available?

Upon exiting the plane, the passengers were handed a ticket and told to wait patiently and they would be helped. The flight was officially not going anywhere, and they were told to make other arrangements, although later in the night the flight attendant at the desk told them that the plane flew to Charlotte at 8:30. Now everyone who knows these two women also knows that patience is not one of their virtues. They quickly agreed that waiting for help from the airline was not a prudent action to take, so they whipped out their smartphones and began searching websites and placing calls to the travel agency through which the flights had been booked. There was much consternation and despair on the part of the passengers of this grounded flight. Melanie and Harriet had several conversations with other people who were trying to make other arrangements for their travel. One attractive dark-haired woman was trying to get to Charlotte for a meeting. She wore an Auburn button on her lapel. Her boss had really wanted her to be in Charlotte on Saturday, but her son played football for Vanderbilt and was a senior. She had stayed in

Birmingham to see him play in the bowl game that had taken place the afternoon before and now she really needed to get to Charlotte on Sunday.

There was no help forthcoming from the onsite airline agents. Nothing was available for a flight to Dallas. Harriet and Melanie began the first barrage of phone calls to airlines and the booking agency through which the original flight had been booked. What did people do before smart phones? Harriet talked on the phone to the Delta, Southwest, American Airlines, and US Airways agents. Finally in desperation, Harriet started calling to check on charter flights and indeed found a pilot who would fly them to Las Vegas. He said the trip would require a big body plane due to the distance and would accommodate 8 passengers. The price for said trip would be $32,000, one-way. Harriet yelled out and asked if there were any parties interested in splitting the cost and the plane ride, but there were no takers.

Then Melanie and Harriet began to walk out of the boarding area with the other discouraged travelers and back into the airport ticket counter area. The lady whose son played for Vanderbilt checked in with her "Auburn buddies" and Harriet told her in a very confident manner, "We are going to make it!" It was about that time that Harriet, once again, was accosted by a total stranger who wondered if she was going to the game in Pasadena. She responded affirmatively, although at that particular time she had no idea how she was going to get there, and then the stranger introduced himself as Torris Babs, an Auburn football letterman. Torris had a friend, Suzanne, who lived in the Los Angeles area and he wanted Harriet to deliver tickets for the championship game to her. He showed her a picture of Suzanne and the lady appeared to be very elderly and looked as though she wouldn't have been able to ride a

14

bus to the Rose Bowl much less sit through a ballgame. Harriet told Torris that she would deliver the tickets, but at the present time had no way to get to California. Harriet also told Torris that her son was a letterman and then told him that she needed to check with ticket agents to see what could be done about the current situation in which she and Melanie found themselves and excused herself from the conversation. Meanwhile Melanie was standing in line at one airline ticket counter then another trying to find a flight that would get them anywhere near their final destination. Of course there were many other Auburn faithfuls who were frantically trying to find a way to Pasadena, too.

It may have been about this time that Courtney called Harriet to check on their progress and the news had to be broken to her that the two sisters were still in Birmingham. Near hysteria ensued as Courtney digested the fact that her mother and aunt were not well on their way to Las Vegas. Courtney calmed herself, and rallied her forces and friends with whom she was having a pre-game party. So, Courtney, Tootie, Renee', Buzzy and a host of others began rooting for the sisters to find a way to get to the game. The prospect of getting a flight was slim to none, but no one was willing to admit that.

What if Batman was about to go on a mission to prevent the Riddler from committing a heinous crime and when he got to the Batcave couldn't find the keys to the Batmobile? Would he have just gone back upstairs to the library and forgotten about the mission?

Melanie and Harriet began working on a solution to their problem and tag-teamed the ticket agents for all airlines. Nothing was available. Everyone in the airport was desperate. As Harriet was passing from one ticket counter to another, Torris was always looming in the periphery. He called friends of his in Dallas to see if they could somehow come up with a solution. As Melanie and Harriet suggested flights out of Jackson, MS, Mobile, Montgomery, Orlando, and Atlanta, to any point west of the Rockies, Torris offered to drive them to the departure point if they would just deliver the tickets to Suzanne when they reached California. The two ladies and Torris were allies with a common goal....passage to the Rose Bowl. At one point in the evening, Torris brought his lettermen's directory over to Harriet with the pages open to the listing for Larkin, her son, and said, "Your son's name is Larkin Deason!" In the midst of the frustration she was experiencing, it was all that she could do to keep from telling him that she was already very aware of her own son's name and that he could never know the countless times her fingers had traced lovingly over those letters and numbers in the lettermen's directory that created the listing, "Larkin Deason, OG, Sprott, 1998-00".

Soon, the airport began to empty out as the last flights for the day landed and then the planes went off to other destinations. Harriet did feel compelled to tell more than one airline employee that it seemed wasteful for a whole crew and airplane that had been prevented from flying to Charlotte to be left sitting on the runway when there were so many people who would gratefully hop on that plane for a flight to Dallas. The comment was ignored. Torris Babs told Harriet that he was leaving and asked if she would contact him if somehow they were successful in getting a flight out on Monday. She took his card and gave him her number and email address. Melanie leaned over and whispered to Harriet, "Who is that dude and what does he want?"

As the crowd thinned, Harriet once again made her way to the US Airways ticket counter with Melanie right behind her. Harriet was trying to get the attention of a ticket agent when they were accosted by a young male who appeared to be from the Middle East. He was complaining that he had missed his flight and the airline was not going to pay for a room for him for the night and the young man apparently wanted them to be sympathetic to his current situation. The two women quickly let him know that while his plight was sad; they had no time for sympathy, because at the current time, they had more desperate issues to resolve. You see, he did not have to be somewhere the next day for THE ball game and they had more important matters to discuss with the ticket agent than he did. Harriet was able to get the attention of a US Airways ticket agent. Her name was Marie. Harriet told Marie that she and her sister really had to get to Pasadena for the BCS game. The window of time had already passed in which they would have been able to make the trip to Vegas to catch the bus out to Pasadena the next day so they set their sights on California. (*"California dreamin' on such a winter's day"*). Marie told her that it might take a miracle and Harriet replied that she believed in miracles and asked Marie if she did. Marie said that she did believe in miracles and that is when the magic began. Marie Webb and Joe Worsham, another ticket agent, started working on finding a flight to Dallas and beyond. They were on the phone for over an hour with Sean at the corporate office.

During this lull while they were waiting to hear back from the ticket agents, Melanie decided to contact Travelocity to cancel the Las Vegas hotel and find out if they could get a refund on the cancelled flights. Since she has difficulty hearing on the phone (or anywhere else, Harriet says), she went outside to find a quiet place only to be blasted by a

17

frigid rain. It was dark and it was cold and she could not understand the agent on the other end of the line very well at all since he had a very heavy foreign accent. So she ran back into the airport, gave the phone to Harriet and asked her to attempt communication with the travel agency's foreign help desk. Not much useful information was gained other than the hotel reservations could not be cancelled until proof of flight cancellations was received by the hotel from the agency. Confused and still wondering if they would get to Pasadena, the two plugged in their phones to prepare for whatever awaited them. Melanie went back downstairs in the airport lobby to the wonderful drink machine that accepted credit cards and purchased another Sierra Mist for them to accompany the chocolates from Courtney's goody bag.

Finally, the lights dimmed in the airport and there were only four travelers left in the ticketing area. No one knows what happened to the young Middle Easterner who had no hotel room. The other two people who were in the area were an odd couple. The young lady was from the LA area and was providing very helpful information for how the two ladies could get from the airport to the Rose Bowl if they ever actually arrived in LA. She even offered to provide them with transportation if she could get her flight changed. There was some weirdness about the young fellow who was with her. The girl had visited Birmingham, Trussville actually, to meet her boyfriend's parents. Well, this young man was not her boyfriend, and his relationship to the young lady was never really explained. It was about that time that the two sisters pulled out their cosmetic bags in order to take advantage of the power of red lipstick. Unless you have personally experienced the sensation, you cannot fully understand the total transformation that a fresh coat of red lipstick can provide. Lipstick should never be underestimated as it has magical powers to refresh and energize the person who applies it on their parched and pale lips.

Joe and Marie beckoned the two women over to the ticket counter. They had done it!!! Somehow, through what seemed like an eternity, they managed to get the two old girls booked on flights. They were so proud of this seemingly impossible feat. Marie told Melanie that she had been able to get two brothers on the last flight out of Birmingham to the championship game in Arizona in 2011 and she was thrilled that she had gotten these two sisters booked for passage to this game. There were hugs and smiles all around and the airline agents were thanked profusely by the grateful, yet very tired sisters.

The planned route that had been miraculously contrived by Marie and Joe was circuitous. The flight would leave Birmingham early on Monday; fly to Dallas, then to Tucson, then to Phoenix, then to Burbank. They would cross into Pacific Time Zone, then back into Mountain Time Zone, then back into Pacific Time Zone before reaching their final destination. The final plane was scheduled to arrive in beautiful downtown Burbank at 3:55 PST which would leave over an hour for Melanie and Harriet to get to the stadium for the game. Life was good!

There was then the decision about whether or not to leave the airport. The weather continued to deteriorate and had turned bitterly cold and freezing rain was predicted for the wee hours of Monday morning. There was some concern about whether or not getting back to the airport on Monday morning would be possible. Melanie and Harriet thought they might need to stay put, but then also realized that they needed to eat, bathe, and change clothes before departing on their morning flight, because there would be no other opportunity for that in the hours ahead. Before leaving the

19

airport, they thanked the young traveler from LA for the information, offered her some chocolate from their stash, and bade her farewell. Harriet emailed Torris to let him know they would return to the airport at 5:00 the next morning and if he could meet her there to hand over the tickets, she would deliver them to his friend in California. Then, Melanie and Harriet got into a cab and went to the Sheraton at the Birmingham Jefferson County Civic Center for a bath and short nap.

They arrived there at 11:00, just as room service ended, so they went down to the bar and had a quesadilla and a drink and watched the end of the Arkansas State ballgame on TV which seemed like a good omen. It may have been just before they went to the bar that Melanie received a call letting her know that the morning flight was going to be delayed. After careful calculations the two women decided that they would still be able to make connections and all was still well. Courtney continued to call with support and helpful tips and was spared this news when she called just after this last bit of information had been received. Around 12:30 a.m., another call came to let Melanie know that the morning flight had been cancelled. Without skipping a beat, Melanie and Harriet whipped out their phones and began to search for a solution. In short order they had 4 tickets for a flight out of Montgomery to Dallas which would be leaving at 6:55 a.m. The only problem was that they had no way to get to Montgomery because both of their cars were locked inside the fence at Warrior Tractor Company. So, they did the only thing they could do. They called Cleve and asked him to come rescue them.

They took a bath and got dressed for the BCS National Championship Game at 1:30 a.m., January 6. They yearned longingly for some time to sleep in the two queen sized beds filled with fluffy pillows and covered in white

sheets and soft coverlets, but they were only able to lie
down for just a few minutes in those early morning hours.
Not that they were able to lie down long enough to have
even the tiniest nap, just long enough to appreciate the
wonderful comfort and softness of the beds.

While waiting for Cleve to arrive, Melanie and Harriet
sorted through their four bags, and repacked into two bags
only the essential items they would need the following day,
actually it was now the same day that they would need
these things for the game. The other bags would be left
with Cleve. This was a traumatic experience as each item
was carefully considered for the final leg of the trip West.
Each item that went into the bag would have to be taken
with them into the Rose Bowl. There was no room for any
extra jewelry, and only room for minimal makeup. Serious
sacrifices were made for this journey. Not even a spare
pair of shoes could accompany them. However, the true
blue navy blue shakers made the cut.

Now I must comment here on the patience that Cleve
exhibited when he received the call that morning. How
many husbands, awakened in the wee hours of a dreadfully
cold morning with freezing rain pelting down, would agree
to make the trip back to Birmingham to pick up his wife
and sister-in-law, drive them to Montgomery to catch an
early morning flight, then drive back to Birmingham and
work all day? I would say that some might have done it,
but no one else would have done it without a great deal of
complaining and arguing. Cleve, however, never raised the
question of why the sisters were determined to continue
their trek or why they thought the three of them should be
motoring about the central portion of Alabama in the midst
of a winter storm in order for them to catch a flight to
Dallas. He had known and loved the two women for more
than forty years and had a good understanding of how they

21

made plans and stuck with them, so he knew there was no need to question them about this plan or offer alternate solutions. When Harriet called and asked him to come pick them up, he just said that he would be there in about an hour and a half. Cleve arrived at the hotel around 3:00 a.m. and because he had driven through freezing rain and very low temperatures, the car doors were frozen shut and there was ice caked all over the Ford Flex, whose car name was Brown Betty.

Brown Betty was not a flashy car, but she was sturdy and steady. She had been on many exciting and fun trips. Brown Betty had carried Melanie and Harriet to Jacksonville only last May to see Melanie's middle grandson graduate from high school. He's the one who became a Seminoles fan. Brown Betty had been to Atlanta for the Kick-Off Classic in 2012 and the SEC Championship game in 2013 and before that had gone with a whole crowd of folks to Knoxville. She drove almost the entire length of the world's longest yard sale only last summer. But most importantly, Brown Betty goes with Harriet to Tuscaloosa every day to the University of Alabama where Harriet works in the library, and then carries her back home safe and sound each night. Even on that awful night of April 27 in 2011, when tornadoes rampaged through the entire southeast and left hundreds dead and untold devastation and destruction in their paths, she carried Harriet safely home. They had to wait patiently in traffic that night while the roads were being cleared of debris tossed onto them by the monster tornadoes, but they finally arrived safe and sound in Sprott. And now, she would take these folks to the airport in Montgomery. She had not been there before.

At some point before Cleve arrived, Courtney called again, ever supportive and loving, and she was told the latest upheaval in the plan. She was assured that all was well, the two sisters would arrive in Beautiful Downtown Burbank with time to spare to reach the Rose Bowl. Courtney had tried to persuade a friend of hers to fly the sisters to California in his plane, but that didn't pan out. Melanie and Harriet had planned to take Cleve back to his truck at Warrior and drive themselves to Montgomery, but Cleve said that he would drive them to the airport. Melanie sent up a silent prayer of thanks for Cleve's generosity and support that night. She and Harriet were thankful that because of Cleve's cooperative spirit, this plan appeared to be going down without a hitch.

Montgomery

So Cleve drove down I65 from Birmingham toward Montgomery in the frigid temperatures and icy rain with the two in tow. Melanie and Harriet had salvaged a bottled drink from somewhere, the airport, I think, and mixed themselves a little "toddy" for the trip with one of the miniatures Courtney had given them. Harriet drifted in and out of a nap, sometimes awakening herself by talking in her sleep or laughing about something she was dreaming about, Melanie was texting and maybe napping. During one of her lucid moments, Harriet emailed Torris Babs to let him know they had abandoned Birmingham and were on their way to Montgomery. She told him that she would not be at the airport that morning, but suggested that he look for a friend of hers, Shane Lee, from Marion, who would be there to fly out of Birmingham on one of the chartered flights. She suggested that Shane would be a good prospect for delivering the tickets to Suzanne. Cleve drove on and they arrived in Montgomery around 5:00 a.m. where Cleve bade them farewell once again. They trudged into the almost empty airport in Montgomery and began their wait for the departure of the 6:55 a.m. flight to Dallas. Melanie called to report to Frank that after almost 24 hours of attempting to get to Las Vegas, she was now in Montgomery approximately 30 miles from where she began her trip on Sunday morning. The first words out of Frank's mouth were "I'm not surprised." He learned long ago that when Melanie leaves the house on an adventure, anything can happen and usually does.

The world was back on a normal keel. The earth had righted itself and once again was spinning properly on its axis. The stay at the Montgomery airport was almost routine. Harriet did get impatient with the ticket agent who did not show up at the ticket counter at the time designated on the sign that was propped up nearby. They snapped at each other rather sharply when the ticket agent announced that she didn't open until 6:00 and Harriet responded that she needed to change the sign because it said that the counter opened at 5:30. After proceeding through security, the two sisters went to the gate and got their boarding passes. They bought breakfast at a small shop and ate it while sitting at the gate. They took pictures of their downsized luggage and posted it on Facebook. Harriet received an email from Torris Babs letting her know that he had connected with Shane Lee at the airport in Birmingham and Shane had agreed to deliver the tickets to Suzanne in LA. The plane took off without any problems. Melanie slept some on the way to Dallas and Harriet rested comfortably in a seat on the front row on the right side of the plane with Melanie in the row behind her. There were others who had waited with them in Montgomery that were also on their way to Los Angeles for the game. A pilot was headed to Los Angeles to pick up a plane for a customer and then fly it back to Montgomery. He was going to the game if he could make all the connections. A woman had decided at the last minute to fly out and join her family members who flew to Los Angeles a few days before. Perhaps they made it all the way, but probably not. When they deplaned in Dallas, Harriet wished them well and made plans to share a cab to the Rose Bowl if they arrived in Burbank at the same time.

Dallas (Big D, little a, double l, a, s)

The plane arrived in Dallas at the scheduled time and Melanie and Harriet made their way into the terminal. And that is where the peace and tranquility that had been experienced since arriving in Montgomery came to a screeching halt. When Melanie got off the plane and got inside the airport, she immediately went to the electronic schedule boards to check the gate for the next flight on their itinerary, and there she saw the worst news possible. The flight to Tucson had been cancelled, and the flight from Tucson to Phoenix had been cancelled. The feeling inside when she saw that sign was like falling down and having the breath knocked out of your body. Harriet joined her and saw the same bad news. So there they stood, looking up at the sign. NO! NO! NO! How could this be happening? It was as if the Gates of Hell had opened up and they were being sucked into the fiery cauldron of the underworld, BUT, they refused to go. At that moment, Harriet wondered why the font on the screen that announced the cancellation of flights was colored green. It should have been BLACK, large looming ominous letters that bespoke the damnation and end to all plans and journeys. If a tear had splashed over the eyelashes and trickled down the cheeks of either of them, the whole trip would have ended right there in a deluge of tears and sobs. They both stood firm, staring at the screen, stubbornly refusing to accept the fate that was spelled out in the green letters there; the green letters that so innocuously stated: Tucson-Cancelled.

So, what was the next step? Without skipping a beat, the two walked over to the US Airways counter and asked how they were supposed to get out of Dallas. They were instructed by the person at the airline counter to go to the re-ticketing counter which was about 20 gates further down the hallway inside the terminal. Harriet took off down the corridor at a slow lope, while Melanie called the booking agency to see if there were other options and in the meantime was roaming through nearby gates checking on standby status for flights to Phoenix. It was at these times during the trip, when they were walking and trudging along the cold corridors between gates that they laughed and said, "This is why we work hard in the Sprang." When Harriet arrived at the re-ticketing gate, there were at least 100 would-be passengers ahead of her. She stood in line for a while then decided that it was futile and senseless to wait for assistance from the ticket agents. By the time she got to the counter to speak to an agent, it would be too late to catch a plane that would arrive in LA in time to see the game. Melanie had just been told by the ticketing agent on the phone the closest they could get them to LA was Fresno and that was 5 hours from the Rose Bowl. She and Melanie had to come up with another plan.

Did the Union Army prevent Scarlett O'Hara from reaching Tara once she made up her mind that she had to get there?

It was do or die time. They had no flight to California. They had no flight to get back home. Would they spend the rest of the day in the airport, call Frank Jr. who lives in Ft. Worth to rescue them OR suck it up one more time, pull out the smart phones, the credit cards and the cash and find a way to get there! They did not have to say it, they just looked into each other's eyes and the decision was made. The Team of Destiny II had not come this far to back down now. They took an oath to get there because, to paraphrase Pat Dye, "Ain't no easy way in life baby!" While Melanie was calling the booking agency to ensure that the flights for their return trip from LA had not been cancelled, Harriet noticed an abandoned seating area in a corner near the re-

27

ticketing counter and walked over and sat down. She began searching again for flights to Los Angeles. There was a link to CheapOAir.com and she called the number listed there. A young man answered the phone and she blurted out, "I need 2 seats from Dallas to Los Angeles, and I have to get there before 5:30 today!" The conversation was difficult because the young man was obviously sitting in a thatched-roof bure on the beaches of a Fijian island with a typhoon roaring in. He was speaking very excitedly and in an accent that was impossible to understand. So, in order to compensate for her inability to understand what the young man was saying, Harriet decided to speak a little louder herself and hoped that would solve the problem. It was an old trick she had learned from Leigh Pegues when she worked for him at Judson College--but that is another story for another day.

Finally, the young man announced he had two seats on a flight to LA. He very meticulously described the extremely good value of the tickets and Harriet asked several questions to ensure there was no way the flight was about to be cancelled. After receiving the answers she sought, Harriet "pulled the trigger" and told the agent to book the flights. This was after she had sign-languaged and mouthed the offer to Melanie who was by that time standing over her in the chair. Melanie had given the ok to proceed with the purchase of the tickets. But, to Harriet's horror, the agent announced that the two tickets had been purchased. But, he asked Harriet to hold for what seemed to be an unusually long time while he searched for other options. Hope was drifting away from her like the air from a deflating balloon, but then the barely understandable voice came over the phone again to say he had two tickets, and Harriet yelled, "I'll take them!" The young man felt obligated to go over every detail, while Harriet continued to yell, "I'll take them, I'll take them!" He wanted to be certain that she understood that one ticket was at a higher price than the other and Harriet once again yelled, "I'll take them!" Then, the ticket agent and Harriet very patiently went through the process of getting the personal information of the two travelers entered into the system. Harriet called upon her daughter's days at Marion Military Institute to remember the code names for the alphabet as she carefully spelled out her name and Melanie's name using the terms Echo, Alpha, etc. It all sounded very official. The guy in Fiji was somehow able to get it all entered correctly. Then it was time to give him the credit card number. As excited as Harriet had been about landing the tickets, she was a little concerned about having to scream out her credit card number in the airport, albeit in a rather secluded, non-populated alcove, but nevertheless, scream it she did and at last, two tickets on a flight that would get them to LA were once again a reality and their itinerary, although slightly modified, was still intact.

Never underestimate the power of two determined women who are holding a fist-full of cash and credit cards.

Now while on the phone with the agent, one of the many questions that Harriet asked the young man was "Where is the Virgin America Airlines gate located in the Dallas/Ft. Worth airport?" He very carefully explained that it was in terminal "E" at Gate zewhoa (zero) two. So off the sisters flew to the airport tram and they giggled as they hustled along and one of them said, or perhaps they both said it simultaneously, "Ain't no easy way in life, Baby! This is why we work hard in the Sprang!" The tram zipped them around the airport to terminal "E" and they got off at the location that would take them directly to gate "Zewhoa Two". They marched right up to gate E02 and Harriet announced that they needed a boarding pass as she showed her ID and confirmation number to the ticket agent. The ticket agent very courteously asked her if she had a passport. It was at that point that Harriet assumed the worst possible thing must have occurred. She must have fallen asleep, Rip Van Winkle style, and awakened many years later in a place where Dallas, or perhaps Los Angeles, was no longer a part of the United States and a passport was required for passage from one place to the other which was now a foreign country. Melanie assumed the worst as well and immediately sputtered, "Damn, we've been scammed!" I can certainly understand why she might have thought that what with the reservations having been made through a website called CheapOAir.com. Then Harriet came to her senses and blurted out, "We're only going to Los Angeles." It was then that the ticket agent kindly informed them that the flight that would be boarding soon from that gate was to Toronto and they were standing at the Air Canada gate. They asked if she knew where they might find the Virgin America Airlines gate and she pointed down the long corridor and said she thought it was in that direction.

It reminded them of the response from the mouse with the pea in her mouth when Peter Rabbit was trying to get out of Mr. McGregor's garden.

So, off they went, with their game day bags in tow which were packed with makeup, underwear, pajamas, and wallets, along with a few other essentials. Harriet's bag also contained two true blue navy blue shakers for the game. Maybe I should tell you a little about their pajamas. Melanie's were turquoise and black jaguar print and Harriet's were purple flannel with sock monkeys playing with balls of yarn printed all over them. It was a wise move for the two ladies to keep these safely hidden in the game day bags. But, Lord, what a pair they would have been if they had chosen to walk through the airport wearing them. But we must get back to the business at hand. They finally made it to gate E20 (not E02), which was the Virgin America Airlines gate. There was not a ticket agent in sight. But, there was a large group there that appeared to be waiting for something, so they decided to sit there and wait with them.

There was a little time to spare before the flight was scheduled to leave, so Melanie asked Harriet if she wanted something to eat. Harriet said "I just want a hotdog". Melanie replied that she had not seen any place along the way down the corridor that sold hotdogs, but Harriet said again, "I just want a hotdog." Melanie rather carefully asked what Harriet might possibly consider eating in the event there were no hotdogs to be found. Harriet once again replied "I just want a hot dog." So Melanie took off down the corridor in search of food (i.e. hotdogs) while Harriet guarded their belongings at the gate. Melanie found "Annie's Pretzels" and decided they might have hotdogs for sale or a reasonable facsimile which would meet Harriet's request and sure enough, they sold pretzel dogs. Now, Melanie was not quite prepared for the difficulties that would ensue while she attempted to make the purchase. Remember they were now in Texas and the shop was manned by a team whose communication skills in English were sorely challenging. Have you noticed a theme here? Melanie noticed a sign that stated that the day's special was two pretzel dogs and a medium drink. She ordered two pretzel dogs and two Diet Cokes. The response she received, was, "Si, you want special?" Melanie explained that she did not really want the special, per se, but instead wanted two hot dogs and TWO Diet Cokes. They went back and forth for a while, until Melanie said, "Look, I want a pretzel dog and a Diet Coke." After paying for that, she ordered another pretzel dog and Diet Coke. By this time there was a line backing up at the pretzel counter and Melanie muttered to several people who were standing nearby that they were out of luck unless they wanted today's special but they could try to order something else if they felt lucky. Melanie returned to the waiting area at the Virgin America Airlines gate with two pretzel dogs and two Diet Cokes, and the pair immediately began eating and drinking. The meal tasted like the food of the gods. It had been a long time since they had eaten at the airport in Montgomery. Little did they know how long it would be before they would eat again.

It may have been at this point that Harriet texted Courtney and asked her to pray that they would make it to the game. Courtney texted her prayer back. It went like this, "Dear sweet Baby Jesus, in your tiny, precious, golden diaper, please let my Mama get to the game tonight. Amen."

Finally, a ticket agent appeared at Gate E20, and Harriet and Melanie almost knocked other passengers down as they vaulted over to the counter. But, they could not get their boarding passes into their hot little hands because there was a glitch with the computer printer. Could this glitch affect their ability to get on that plane? Oh, good Lord! Please say it ain't so! The ticket agent promised he would let them know just as soon as the printer was working again. And he did. When Melanie and Harriet again approached the ticket counter, trying not to knock others down as they hurriedly stepped past them, Harriet whipped out her phone to get the confirmation numbers. Now when I said she whipped it out, I really meant that she dug through her bag for a while, set a few things out onto the counter, and then, while trying not to dump out her underwear and pajamas, finally fished it out of the bottom of the bag (aforementioned game day bag). There was Melanie's confirmation number in an email, but even though Harriet knew she had seen both confirmations, her confirmation was not to be found at that time. She totally freaked out and Melanie reassured her that she would not leave without her if she couldn't find the confirmation. As it turned out, the ticket agent only needed their ID's and not the confirmation numbers, so gleefully, they slapped their driver's licenses down onto the counter, two boarding passes were printed, and once again, the two sisters were in business. Of course, Harriet's confirmation was right there at the top of the screen on her phone as soon as she returned to her seat. They both sat down to wait and applied another coat of lipstick.

People were already eating and drinking on the grounds of the Rose Bowl getting ready to go into the stadium and there they were trying to stay warm in DFW. But, a calm descended over the pair once again. They had faced the dragon and slew it—almost. Just a quick flight to San Francisco, a change of planes, then onto their final destination, LA, and the prize would be theirs. Well, almost, there would still be a ride in the taxi to the Rose Bowl. At that point, they were at peace with their accomplishment and decided that if they didn't get to the game before it was over, they would still go to the Rose Bowl and have their picture taken in front of it—no matter what time they arrived in LA.

I should mention here that calls and texts, filled with encouragement, love, concern, and possible flight connections continued to pour in almost continuously from Courtney. The two sisters' trials, triumphs and tribulations were now being followed by a number of Courtney's friends who had gathered in Greensboro to watch the game and other friends and family who were following their progress on Facebook and via phone and text messages. They were closely approaching the status of folk heroes and were being cheered onward toward their goal of arriving in Los Angeles to attend the championship game.

California

The time finally arrived to board the plane to San Francisco and it was totally booked. Melanie boarded first, and after a long wait Harriet got a little concerned that there might not be room on the plane for her, but finally she got on and took her seat on the plane, which was right behind Melanie's seat. I must interject at this point that Harriet and Melanie had matching shawls/wraps which had been made from blue and orange tiger stripe fleece by Harriet prior to the trip. They had proven to be very versatile thus far during the trip and would now serve as a combination blanket and pillow for this leg of the journey. They believed that the matching shawls were instrumental in garnering attention from U.S. Airways ticket agents in Birmingham and may have been what caused them to work so diligently to get the pair a flight to LA. These same shawls had caused several comments and questions from other passengers in Dallas most of whom were under the mistaken impression the two women were returning from the Bengals game which had been played the day before. What was wrong with these people? Did they not know the BCS Championship game was to be held that very day, in a matter of hours, and that the sisters' very own AUBURN TIGERS were playing? Did I mention that the shawls had fringe all around the edges?

If it would have made the plane go any faster, they would have pushed it down the runway or flapped their arms like wings, or lifted their feet off the floor. There was nothing to do but wait for the long flight to begin and then end. And so the fully-packed plane taxied out and flung itself down the runway and up, up, up, into the afternoon sky. Of course there was no way to see the afternoon sky because this airline catered toward the younger generation and all window flaps were snugly closed and lavender lighting

illuminated the interior of the aircraft. Melanie made a
mental note to check on Virgin America flights from now
on when she had to travel.

They were both exhausted, and Melanie shared with Harriet
one of the orange and white polka dot bags that Courtney
had filled with chocolate. It would have been polite to have
offered one of the chocolates to their fellow travelers sitting
beside them, but air travel is not a polite affair these days.
It is much more like riding a bus from Dallas to
Montgomery in the 1960's. Maybe it is more casual than
that, because nowadays most people dress as if they are
going to bed instead of going on an exciting journey.
Perhaps the sisters should have worn their pajamas for the
flight to San Francisco. Melanie and Harriet did ride a bus
in the early sixties from Selma to Montgomery, but there
was nothing casual about that trip. Their mother had
gussied them up in their Sunday best and deposited them on
the seat directly behind the driver with strict instructions on
how they were to behave on their short journey and strict
instructions to the driver regarding his responsibility to care
for and protect her daughters. Their father's cousin, Lee
Hartley, her husband J.M., and their three children met
Melanie and Harriet at the Continental Trailways depot in
downtown Montgomery later that afternoon. Melanie and
Harriet rode the bus to Montgomery so they could attend
the Southeastern Livestock Exhibition, otherwise known as,
"the rodeo". The guest celebrities at the rodeo were the
actors who played Rowdy Yates and Wishbone on the
popular TV show, "Rawhide". The actor who portrayed
the dashing and daring Rowdy Yates each week was Clint
Eastwood. The two sisters made their way back to Sprott
with an autographed 8x10 photo of him, which Melanie
hung onto through the years, along with the ticket stub
from the 1963 Florida State game. There would be no
autographs requested on this flight to San Francisco and no

35

one would be concerned that their frilly little frock was going to get wrinkled along the way.

Harriet was very concerned about the time that their flight would actually land in San Francisco and if the schedule would get them there in time to catch the flight to LA. Boarding the plane took a very long time because the flight was so full, and then there was the hassle at the ticket counter between the agents and a family of three who believed they had tickets, but only had an itinerary, all causing delays, delays, delays. Harriet wondered if the tickets that had been intended for the family had become her ticket and Melanie's ticket by some stroke of fate. Then, the TSA showed up and had a full-scale search of everyone who boarded the plane. Could the last minute purchase of tickets from CheapOAir.com have prompted the search? Because of the time delays in departing Dallas, Harriet asked one of the flight attendants about their arrival time in San Francisco and whether there would be sufficient time to make the connection for the next leg of their journey. The attendant was serving drinks at the time, but she said she would check on it.

There was a monitor on the back of each seat in the plane which allowed the passengers to play games, view TV and movies, and place orders for food. As they threw back a considerable quantity of miniature Snickers and Heath bars from the orange and white polka dot bags, Melanie and Harriet watched ESPN and all of the hoopla that preceded the BCS Championship Game on the little monitors. Also, and perhaps more importantly, on the screen a person could see the map of their current journey with a picture of a little plane that showed their exact location on the map. The air speed and altitude of the plane were also displayed on that screen. Harriet watched this for a while, determined that they were indeed headed toward the west coast, and then drifted off into a restless nap. Meanwhile, Melanie tried to nap while she held the orange polka dot bags with the remaining chocolates in her lap. This was a mistake. When Harriet awoke she thought that surely they were almost ready to land in San Francisco. But, to her horror the little plane on the screen was still laboriously struggling to get across New Mexico. There was still another 700+ miles to travel before landing in San Francisco. Good Lord, how far had it been to begin with? Was San Francisco on the other side of the world? Would the trip require that they circumnavigate the globe? About that time the flight attendant stopped by to assure Harriet that the flight would land in San Francisco with plenty of time to catch the other plane that would take them to LAX. LAX was not the preferred airport for the trip. Burbank would have been much closer to the Rose Bowl, but it was impossible to get a flight to Burbank that day from Dallas. So, they missed their opportunity to visit Beautiful Downtown Burbank as it was referred to on the TV show, Laugh-In, in the 1960's.

Melanie woke up to discover that the last few pieces of chocolate in the orange and white polka dot bag had melted as she held them in her lap, but with some effort she and Harriet were able to scrape the chocolate from the wrappers and finish it off. As Harriet watched the little plane on the monitor, it eventually flew over the mountains and began its final approach toward San Francisco. Closer and closer the little plane on the screen moved toward the final destination, until finally she felt the big bird with lavender interior lighting floating downward toward the airport.

Harriet thought that it would be more practical and expedient if the airlines created a policy that would allow those passengers who did not attempt to stuff everything they owned into the overhead compartments of the airplane the opportunity to deplane first. With this not being the case, she and Melanie prepared to quickly make their way off the plane. Somehow, they managed to make a fairly quick exit before all of the other folks came to their senses and started shuffling about. They rapidly walked out of the plane, up the jet way, into the airport and straight to the restroom. This would be their final opportunity to put on more makeup and make one last futile attempt to re-do their hair. I should mention here that Melanie had been battling an infection of her tear duct throughout the trip and she had to carefully manage how long she kept her contacts in her eyes, so she was switching back and forth from glasses to contacts. But, her hair was in good shape, Harriet's—not so good. Melanie determined at this stop that it was time to put the contacts in for game time. So, with a change of contacts, an extra coat of make-up, a fresh application of lipstick, and a final tweak to the hair, they walked out of the restroom and to their surprise, their flight to Los Angeles was already boarding. They quickly got in line and in a matter of minutes were in their seats. The plane had very few passengers, so they were able to sit wherever they wanted. Even though their seats were not originally assigned together, they chose to sit side-by-side during the final leg of the trip.

As they took off from San Francisco, they could see a long bridge spanning the bay. It might have been the Golden Gate Bridge. No one really knew for sure. Melanie said with some authority that it was the bridge, so it became official; they saw the Golden Gate Bridge. The plane had an unusual amount of energy and strength as it rapidly climbed into the air and above the clouds. This was it! They were going to make it to Los Angeles! It was hard for them to really believe that they were at that moment inside of a plane that would finally get them to Los Angeles. It seemed almost impossible, in fact, only a few hours ago, it <u>had</u> been impossible; yet, here they were, in the air, on their way.

The flight had a surreal quality due to the way the light of the sun glinted and glimmered, first off the water of the bay, then off the rocks of the canyons and hills. As the plane floated higher and higher, constantly climbing as if it was a bird struggling to break free from a tether, the fluffy clouds surrounded them and then the clouds were suddenly below them. The tops of the clouds were washed with the Auburn orange colors of the setting sun and delicately splattered with lighter hues of peach, amber and apricot. The clouds at the horizon were a dark blue. And the mix of the colors of the sky, Auburn orange and blue, created a perfect setting for the final approach to the long sought after destination of the two women. Just as the Auburn team worked hard to get to where they were tonight, so had these two women.

At last, the plane was approaching Los Angeles and the goal was in site. The lights of the city and the hills surrounding it were glowing in the early evening light. Harriet tried to check to see if the freeways appeared to be clogged with the 5:00 p.m. rush hour traffic and they didn't seem to be. She and Melanie were watching ESPN on the little monitor and the Auburn band was marching onto the field. Touch down! The plane was on the ground.

As the choir from Heaven sang The Hallelujah Chorus, they all said, AMEN! AMEN! AMEN!

Harriet never really knew that Melanie could move so fast. They made a quick stop at the restroom and then fairly sprinted out to the taxis. Do you remember the commercial from years ago when O. J. Simpson was running through airports and leaping over barriers? They were not moving that fast, but they certainly didn't lose any time getting to the line of taxis outside the airport terminal. After a brief conversation with the man at the taxi stand, they piled in and told the driver they needed to get to the Rose Bowl as quickly as possible; the two old ladies had to get to Pasadena.

She drives real fast and she drives real hard, she's the terror of Colorado Boulevard.

I can't describe to you the feeling that the two felt at that moment. Pat Dye might have said that he wasn't smart enough to tell you the way they felt about it and I don't think that I am either. They jubilantly grabbed their phones and began texting and calling to let everyone know that they were on the ground and running, just as fast as they could, to the Rose Bowl. Harriet called Larkin and found out that Larkin and Miller were watching the game. At least Miller was watching it for a while, until he could switch over to Mickey Mouse. Harriet was able to get Miller to do the "Git 'em, git 'em, git 'em," scream that she screamed repeatedly during every ball game. Miller had witnessed this several times and was able to scream it almost as loudly as Ace. Then when Ace (Harriet's grandmother name) told Miller that she was with Aunt Melanie, Miller responded by yelling "Aunt Mewonee! He then demanded that he get to talk to Aunt Mewonee and everyone was laughing and talking and having a great time. Melanie called and texted her grandsons, Kevin, Brandon and Drew, her son Michael, and her husband Frank. Michael was on active duty on an aircraft carrier in the middle of the Persian Gulf at the time. I'm not certain how thrilled he was to hear the updates about the trip to the game because he is a Bama fan and had not fully recovered from the last second defeat by Auburn on November 30. Brandon, Melanie's grandson, had forgotten she was going to the ballgame, so he was rather surprised to hear that she was in Los Angeles. Harriet called Courtney and screamed, "We're in the cab on the way to the Rose Bowl!" There was much cheering and celebration by those in Greensboro who had been rooting for them. Harriet called Cleve to let him know they were almost there.

The traffic was moving along well and their driver pointed out landmarks as they drove past. They passed by Universal Studios and the venue where the Lakers play basketball. Everything was going well. Larkin was texting play-by-play updates to Harriet as she and Melanie were making their way through Los Angeles. Auburn was ahead! Larkin also called Melanie to remind her of her promise to him to take care of his mother and get her to the Rose Bowl. He stated that she was in danger of being fired from this job unless they picked up the pace. Melanie's promise to him was payback for extracting the same promise from him to care for her sister and get her to the SEC Championship game the month before. He had delivered and now Melanie was expected to do the same.

The taxi driver seemed to be caught up in the excitement and was working as hard as he could to get the two sisters to their destination. Then, all of a sudden, and from out of nowhere, the traffic slowed to a crawl. An electronic sign on the side of the boulevard indicated there had been a wreck somewhere down the road and there would be one-lane traffic ahead. The taxi driver continued to work hard. He swerved and turned off one road and then back onto another until finally they were on Ventura Ave., and then Colorado Boulevard, and then, they knew they were almost there, because there were the Rose Bowl Parade viewing stands that Harriet and Melanie recognized from almost 60 years of watching the parade on New Year's Day.

The cab turned left at the viewing stands and the two sisters realized they had almost made it!!! The cab driver wanted to be certain they could get in touch with him if they needed a ride back and so he gave them his name, which was Asjfar (yes, I think that is correct, he actually spelled it a couple of times so that Harriet could enter it into her phone). Asjfar pulled up as close to the Rose Bowl as the event coordinators would allow him to. He even asked if he could go beyond the barriers, but received a very firm negative response to that question. And so Melanie paid the tab, which with tip was a little over $150, and the two quickly departed the cab with their game day bags and headed to the stadium.

There it was! The Rose Bowl! In living Technicolor! The fabled stadium looked just like it did when they had seen it on TV. It was a throwback to the heyday of Hollywood. THEY HAD MADE IT!!! Melanie lost no time reveling in the view of the Rose Bowl, but immediately set her sights on negotiating the crudely constructed chain link fence around the venue and was looking for a gate, any gate, through which they could enter the Rose Bowl.

Again, Harriet was amazed at the speed at which her sister was travelling on this final leg of their journey. They made their way across the dimly lit, grassy area outside the stadium and as they approached the perimeter of the stadium they realized it had more of the look of a county fair than a football stadium. There was one very unassuming gate at which several security people were standing. The pair determined that must be the entry into the Rose Bowl so they headed in that direction. The security officers told the two late arrivals their bags would have to be searched. The two women responded that they should by all means check their belongings, but they should not expect to find any liquor or food in the bags because if there had been any available liquor or food it would have been consumed long before their arrival at the Rose Bowl. The bags had been x-rayed and searched by multiple cadres of TSA and airport authorities, so this search was not likely to result in a discovery of loot and bounty. The women were very anxious to proceed on into the stadium, so they helped security officers search through the bags and tried to hurry them up as they sorted through pajamas, underwear, and socks.

As the pair of weary travelers got close to Tunnel 27 where according to their ticket they were to enter, a large number of people were exiting the stadium. It was almost halftime. Harriet noticed that a tear had slid down Melanie's cheek. She wasn't sure if it was from pure joy or from the tear duct infection, but neither of them mentioned it and they pushed on. Just outside the tunnel a line of portable toilets stood as if they were soldiers standing at attention. There were some rather defunct concession trailers that appeared to have been recycled from a carnival and then scattered around in front of the tunnel. The sisters forged on in through the crowd and into the Rose Bowl. Of course, Harriet immediately went to the wrong row and had to be redirected to the opposite side of the tunnel, but finally, finally, finally, they had arrived and were seated at THE GAME!

Ever to Conquer, Never to Yield! (or as Harriet's 3-year old grandson would sing that song, War Eagle, Fly up the Hill, Go, Go, Go!).

So there they were—at the Rose Bowl, to see their beloved Tigers play in the BCS Championship Game. Was there ever a doubt about whether or not they would make it? The two sisters could never in a million years have imagined on that November day in 1963 as they sat and watched Auburn play the Florida State Seminoles that they would be sitting in the Rose Bowl on this night 50 years later watching Auburn play the Florida State Seminoles. Only this time, they were playing for the national championship. Surely their grandmother, Faye, was looking down on the two of them and also watching the spectacle before them with a smile on her face.

Their presence at the game started a buzz in the crowd. Somehow people who were sitting near them overheard the sisters saying that they had just arrived after a taxi cab ride from LAX. Several people asked if that was really true and they responded with a wide grin and an affirmative nod. They may have told them, "Ain't no easy way in life, Baby!" But after the initial greetings and moving things around to make room for the late arrivers, the crowd around them behaved in a weird manner. The crowd was aloof in a very un-Auburnly way.

There was about one inch of beer on the floor where they were sitting. But, then there could be an explanation for that. The people who had to hike out to the carnival trailers outside the stadium and wait in line forever before having the opportunity to purchase beer, then had to carry it all the way back into the stadium, may have been entirely too weak to hold on to the cup after such a tortuous ordeal, and then dropped the beer before they had a chance to drink it. It is also entirely possible that in their excitement to get to their seats, Melanie and Harriet knocked over several cups of beer and stepped on the feet of every person sitting on that row. That would have explained the aloofness of their fellow Tigers. Whatever the case, the atmosphere was a little odd. The reason that the beer was a problem at all, really, was that upon sitting down, Harriet reached into her game day bag, pulled out the two true blue navy blue shakers, and immediately dropped them into the beer. She had gotten them at the Clemson game in Atlanta in September 2012, taken them to Auburn and back to Sprott several times, to Knoxville, TN, then to Birmingham, Montgomery, Dallas, San Francisco and finally to Los Angeles. Now, they lay limp in a pool of beer at her feet.

The sisters later decided that they much preferred their Auburn friends who sat with them in section 104 at Jordan-Hare. There were always interesting, happy, friendly Auburn people sitting around them and they all stood and yelled and yelled and yelled during the games. There was the nice man from Tuscaloosa who always asked Harriet if Auburn was going to win and laughed when Harriet told him, "We're going to beat them like a rented mule!" It was so much fun to receive hugs from Brandon Cox when Auburn scored. Brandon's curly-haired friend, who sat nearby, was always very engaged in the game and celebrated wildly when Auburn scored. The sisters learned to be careful in their celebrations with him because he could land a high five that would knock you into the day after tomorrow. So they made sure they had firm footing before engaging in a celebration with him. There was also the cute young blonde girl who pulled the hem of her maxi dress up over her head during one game when things weren't going so well. She said that Melanie and Harriet reminded her of how she and her sister enjoyed being together. Brandon and his buddies enjoyed sharing the miniature bars of Snickers that Melanie packed in her game day bag. Did I ever describe the game day bags? Melanie's bag was laminated and the pattern was orange and blue tiger stripes. The bag had long shoulder straps and a zipper to keep things securely stashed inside. Harriet's laminated bag was blue with large orange polka dots and long straps but only had a little snap at the top to keep all the stuff inside. This, as you can imagine did have its challenges on a given day.

45

As the sisters got settled in, the Auburn band was on the field marching around in their usual fabulous fashion. The two old girls from Sprott made several phone calls and texts to let others know they had arrived. Larkin texted he was exhausted from carrying the weight of pulling Auburn through and was handing over the responsibility to his mother and aunt.

But then, the Rose Bowl came into focus and they began to take in the spectacle inside the "Granddaddy of Them All". It soon became apparent why the Rose Bowl is dubbed "the Granddaddy". It is very old and is showing its age. To put it bluntly, the Rose Bowl is a dump. There were no restrooms inside the stadium at the south end zone. Maybe there were restrooms inside in other areas in the stadium? No concession stands inside either. The atmosphere was more like that of a high school stadium with a county fair and carnival going on outside the stadium than the site of an important collegiate event. The bottom half of the stadium was built down into the ground that had been dug out like a bunker and the top of the bowl stretched out low and wide allowing the sounds from the band and crowd to drift effortlessly over the top bleachers and out toward the San Gabriel Mountains. Maybe Auburn fans are spoiled by a great game day experience in Jordan-Hare, but this was not what the sisters had expected. Harriet leaned over and told Melanie that based on what she had noticed on the way in, they definitely didn't want to be left there alone after the game.

Then the teams ran back out onto the field and the crowd erupted into a roar that floated away into the night. Harriet noticed FSU's mascot, an Appaloosa horse named Renegade, standing just at the corner of the end zone in front of them with Chief Osceola astride. As Harriet looked to her right at the Auburn team she noticed that their shoes and helmets glittered with gold. That was a little strange. A little bit too much Division 1A-ish for the Auburn Tigers in her opinion. Were they going to a dance recital? She thought to herself that there is absolutely nothing wrong with the classic Auburn uniform and it really doesn't need any additives for spark and flair. Not that she is against bling, because bling is her thing when used appropriately and in good taste. However, there is no place for bling on an Auburn football uniform. Melanie was puzzled by the bling on the Auburn uniforms. She thought for some time that what appeared to be bling was only a fuzzy glare that she was seeing due to the tear duct infection. When Harriet commented on the gold stuff on the shoes and helmets, Melanie was a little relieved that it was indeed the glitter of gold that she was seeing and not an apparition. Later, she agreed with Harriet that the gold stuff on the uniforms was totally unnecessary.

At last, the game was going on right there before their eyes. It was magical! During a time out in the third quarter, Harriet leaned over and reminded Melanie that they didn't have a way to leave the Rose Bowl or a place to stay after they left. Just stop for a moment and think about this. Here are these two women from rural Alabama who are 2000 miles away from home with nothing but a few basic necessities, credit cards, some cash, smart phones, and tickets to the BCS game. They have been without sleep for close to 40 hours, have had considerably less food than they normally consume, have no place to sleep that night and wouldn't know how to get there even if they did. But, they were at the game and decided they would worry about hotel accommodations as soon as the game ended. They stood and screamed during the final 2 quarters of the game, and were of course disappointed when Jameis Winston was able to lead FSU down the field in the final seconds to win the game.

The game ended in the end zone right before their very eyes. The Auburn Team of Destiny had given it everything they had and left it all on the field as had the women of the Team of Destiny II. Melanie was reminded of the 1989 Sugar Bowl where she sat in the SuperDome and watched Auburn lose to FSU when Deion Sanders knocked the ball away from Lawyer Tillman in the endzone to end a drive that would have won the game for Auburn. The end of the game reminded Harriet of an unsuccessful attempt to roast marshmallows. You know how that goes; you're standing there with the marshmallow on the stick over the flame, it is perfectly roasted, golden and puffy, then all of a sudden, the whole thing erupts into flames and turns into a charred, gooey mess that falls off the stick and plops into the fire. However, it had been a beautiful, fabulous, wonderful season and even the loss in this championship game could not diminish that.

So, the Tigers were defeated and left the field while the FSU fans stayed and celebrated with their team. During the final minutes of the game, Melanie was able to find out that there were shuttle buses that would transport fans from the stadium to downtown Old Pasadena and it was free of charge. So, that ticked off one of the concerns they had and now they knew how they would get out of the Rose Bowl. Melanie told Harriet that she needed to reserve a room for them, so Harriet found the phone and began searching for a hotel in the area. She couldn't see the screen on her phone very well and realized that her contact had fallen out of her left eye sometime during the day. So, Melanie had to look at the phone and decide on a location, and she used Harriet's phone to dial the number listed. Well, then there was another problem, because Melanie couldn't hear well enough to understand what the person on the other end of the line was saying, so she turned the phone back over to Harriet. Did everyone except the two of them speak with a foreign accent? When it was time for Harriet to give the person who was reserving the room for them her credit card number, she couldn't read the number on the card, so she gave the card to Melanie. Melanie had to read the card number out loud to Harriet, and then Harriet repeated the number in a voice loud enough to be heard over the celebration going on down on the field. And in the midst of golden confetti erupting and falling over everything on the field, loud explosions, speeches, screaming fans, and Renegade prancing in the corner of the end zone, the reservation at the Hilton in Montebello (where was Montebello?) was confirmed and they were set for the remainder of that night and began to make their way out of the Rose Bowl.

As they got outside, they decided that it was time to make a picture of themselves in front of the Rose Bowl. Harriet took a picture of Melanie with the Rose Bowl in the background and then Melanie took a few pictures of Harriet with the Rose Bowl in the background. Later, when they were looking at the pictures, Melanie's picture was perfect, but the only shot that survived of the photo that was to have been of Harriet was a picture of Melanie's thumb.

After the photo session, they wandered over to a security officer to ask where they should go to get on the free shuttle to downtown Pasadena and the officer pointed to a long line that was assembling next to some temporary chain link fencing. The fencing formed a corridor that wound around the carnival concession stands and cinder block buildings. I must mention here that the crew that was working at the game had much that they could have learned from the Bruno Event Team that works at the Auburn games. The crew in Pasadena was rude and very uninformed about what they were supposed to be doing and about what the crowd was supposed to do and where they were supposed to go.

While Melanie and Harriet were waiting in line for the shuttle bus, Melanie realized that she didn't have her Tiger stripe wrap, so she left Harriet in line and went back inside the stadium to get it. But, when she went back in, the shawl was gone; someone had taken it home with them. She went back outside and got in line with Harriet, but not without a brief encounter with one of the event team staff. Someone decided that they were not going to allow her to join Harriet in the line that would lead them to the shuttle buses. Obviously the staffer had no clue about the kind of person she was dealing with. Melanie quickly informed her that was her sister over there in line and she was "INDEED" going over there to join her, and she did. The pair of women stayed in line and slowly made their way through the serpentine alley created by the temporary chain link barriers that marked the way toward the shuttle buses. There were some cars parked randomly beyond the fence and one of the tailgaters had a small campfire burning right beside his car. For some reason the campfire reminded Harriet of the Okies who made their way to California to escape their plight in the Midwest during the years of the Dust Bowl and Great Depression. At other times, in other places, fire so close to a car might have caused the sisters to have been concerned, but at that point, outside the Rose Bowl, after the game, it didn't seem to be the least bit strange, or dangerous. Finally, after more than an hour, and after walking almost the complete circumference of the Rose Bowl, they were closing in on the buses. A man, one of the event crew, was barking out orders to the fans and telling them which bus to get into. He yelled to Harriet, "Hey Tiger lady! Come over here!" And so Harriet and

Melanie headed in that direction and as Harriet was nearing the steps of the bus she turned to the person who was standing behind her and asked him, "Did you drink the Kool-aid, too?"

As luck would have it, Melanie and Harriet got on the bus which was driven by a complete lunatic. The bus moved along at a snail's pace and the trip downtown, though only a 15 minute walk, took more than an hour. As they made their way through the night, other buses zipped past them as their bus lumbered along in the right lane. Melanie pulled out another orange and white polka dot bag and shared the last few pieces of chocolate with Harriet. They hoped this bit of sugar and caffeine would get them through the dreadful journey on the bus. Every time the bus slowed or stopped for a few seconds, Harriet's head immediately fell backward, her mouth fell open and she fell asleep—until, the bus lurched forward again and she awoke and began talking in mid-sentence. Finally the bus ride ended and they disembarked near a parking deck. They hoped to find restaurants nearby that could accommodate a few thousand late night travelers.

It was at this point of the trip that Harriet finally understood a remark from a man in a television news van after the SEC Championship game on December 7. Larkin and Harriet attended the championship game and stayed in the parking lot after the game for a while to celebrate and wait for the traffic to dissipate. When they finally left the parking lot, Michigan State was leading Ohio State. As they were sitting at a traffic light not far from the parking lot, a man in a TV news van honked his horn, rolled down his window and beckoned to Larkin to roll his window down, which Larkin did because all Auburn fans were happy, friendly, and thrilled to be alive that night. The man shouted, "When you go to the Championship Game, stay in Orange

County!" Larkin shouted, "Okay, thanks!" and then rolled up the window.

So, obviously in Orange County, there actually are restaurants and hotels and the like. But, Melanie and Harriet had been put off the bus in a place where there appeared to be little more than a parking deck. So, they began to wander down the street toward a place that looked like it could be promising. Others were headed in the same general direction. At last, they stumbled into a restaurant that was packed slam full of people who had the same intention as theirs. Melanie gave them her name and was told the wait would be about 35 minutes or possibly an eternity, whichever came first. The two decided that they would just stroll a little further down the street during their "35 minutes" of waiting to see if something else might be available. They found a charming little bistro and walked in. It was indeed a beautifully restored or well-maintained little jewel of a building. Inside, the walls and ceilings were sheathed in beautiful carved wood mouldings and paneling. Old, beveled mirrors were imbedded between the wooden panels of dark, well-rubbed wood that bespoke oldness and secrets of many occurrences that had taken place within those walls over the years. The bistro was tiny; very narrow and long. Entering it was like stepping into another world. So, Melanie and Harriet gladly stepped in and took a seat at a small table along the wall to their right as they entered into the bistro. Unfortunately, they were so tired, they were not able to fully appreciate the beauty of the place and at that point they would have been almost as thrilled to be seated in a booth at McDonald's or Denny's. They were greeted very quickly by a person they assumed was the owner, who told them that their server would be with them as soon as possible. The entire staff, although very courteous, did seem to be a little harried by the overrun of guests they had no doubt served during the past few hours. Of course Melanie and Harriet were ready for a drink, but when Melanie ordered a Jack and 7-Up, she was told by the server that they had an "open bar". Now, you must remember that Melanie and Harriet grew up in Perry County, Alabama. And there, if someone mentions an open bar it means that you are attending an event that allows you to be the beneficiary of the generosity of your host and hostess who have provided drinks of all sorts for your consumption. At such an event, you are not only allowed, but expected to consume large quantities of the beverages along with all of the other party fare that is available. So their ears did perk up a bit, but they soon learned the open bar in California was not anything like the open bar to which they were accustomed. When Melanie asked for an explanation about the open bar concept the server told her that they served artisanal beers and wines, and some national brands of beer. Not completely understanding the logic, but totally ready to drink whatever they had to offer, Melanie ordered a beer. Since Harriet was already having some difficulty staying awake, she settled for a Diet Coke.

In addition to the rather strange offering of drinks and terminology, the tiny restaurant had a limited menu to offer to the weary travelers. The ladies were delighted to have found a place that was serving food at that hour (it was about 12:30 a.m. PST), so they cheerfully placed an order. Harriet ordered a cheeseburger and some fries to go with her Diet Coke. Melanie had a burger and fries as well. While they were sitting there waiting for their food to be served, an unfortunate scene occurred at the table next to them. Three Auburn fans were upset about the timing of their service and delivery of food. They stomped out after being very rude to their server. She was visibly shaken by the incident and probably wanted to throw down her apron and run screaming from a nightmarish evening at work.

She was very young and cute, a tiny wisp of a girl with blond hair. She was wearing leggings, a little white shirt, an apron, and some very cute flat shoes. Harriet felt the need to apologize for the behavior of her Auburn comrades.

The wait for their food was long, and so the sisters amused themselves as best they could. There was a large contingent of FSU fans in the place and they had been sitting at the bar drinking whatever it is you drink from a bar that is an "open bar" and they were all feeling pretty happy. The group was chanting FSU cheers and frequently spelled out Florida State and ended that feat with a resounding cheer. Melanie and Harriet agreed that if it had been a group of Bammers sitting there after a game in which they had defeated Auburn, food or no food, hungry or not, they would have left. Somehow, the cheers from the FSU crowd didn't bother them. The FSU fans that Melanie and Harriet encountered were all very nice and very happy and excited.

Just before the food arrived, Harriet realized that she had dozed off while sitting upright in a straight-backed chair in a restaurant while drinking Diet Coke and had awakened herself by talking in her sleep. She was giggling about something in a dream when she woke up. Once awake, Harriet asked Melanie if she had any ideas about how they were going to find a taxi in the wee hours of the morning in what seemed to be a totally deserted sort of place. They chatted about their options and the possibilities for a few minutes and then the conversation lapsed. Harriet leaned over and said the following to Melanie in a loud voice, "I just want you to know that I am having a wonderful time, and I love you, but you and I can't hear each other very well, so I'm not going to talk anymore." Melanie's hearing was not the best before the trip, but after the many flights they had been on, both Harriet and Melanie were suffering from ear conditions that made them feel as though they were listening to each other from the bottom of a well. Their food arrived shortly and they dove in and ate with great delight.

So, as they were finishing their meal, Melanie asked their server if she could suggest a taxi service to call. The young lady with the cute shoes told her they would be able to hail a cab on Colorado Blvd. but she also jotted down the number of a cab company and gave it to Melanie. So, out the door and into the California Night went the two sisters looking for Colorado Blvd. ("She drives real fast and she drives real hard. She's the terror of Colorado Blvd.") They were the two old ladies in Pasadena. Fortunately, Colorado Blvd. was a block away. They easily found a cab that was available for service and piled into the back seat. The two were experts in hailing cabs from their visit to New York City back in 2004 when an undefeated Auburn team was locked out of the championship game. They were there the weekend that Auburn played in the SEC Championship game and could be heard screaming "War Eagle" while standing in the large crowd outside the studio from which the Today Show was being broadcast. They were decked out in full Auburn regalia which included an orange feather boa for each of them.

The driver in Pasadena asked for their destination and Melanie told him the address for the Hilton Hotel at Montebello. The driver just couldn't get the address entered into his GPS system and he was very rude to Melanie as she very patiently spelled out the address and carefully articulated the street number. He consistently entered an "a" for every "e" in the address. The pattern continued – English was not his native language. He then turned and tossed the GPS into Melanie's lap and told her to enter the address into it herself. As you can imagine, that went over like a lead balloon and Harriet opened her door and said "Let's get out of here", which was exactly the same thing that Melanie was thinking as she tossed the GPS back to the rude cab driver. So they both bailed out of the cab and were once again back on the sidewalk.

Very soon, they spotted another cab and the driver told them that he needed to give his friend a ride back home, but they could ride along and then he would drive them to their hotel. At this time of what was now Tuesday morning, and with almost 48 hours without sleep, the two sisters thought this seemed to be a reasonable deal. So, they hopped in and away they went. Well, this cab driver confirmed what they thought might be the case; this was the dumbest bunch of cab drivers they had ever encountered. The cab driver called his dispatch office to get directions to the hotel and after a long conversation hung up, but it was difficult for the two in the back seat to tell whether he really knew where he was going. As they watched the total on the cab meter steadily climb, Melanie yelled to the driver that he had just passed the entrance to the hotel. He didn't seem to believe they had and kept driving down the street. Harriet noticed the amount on the meter and determined that she would not pay more for the ride than the total that was on the meter at that time plus a minimal tip. She shouldn't have left a tip at all, but she didn't want to give this cab driver a reason to sit around talking to his buddies about the two old ladies with the strange accent who turned out to be cheapskates! Melanie finally convinced the driver to turn around and directed him back to the entrance to the golf course where the hotel was located and instructed him on how to get in through the gate. He kept saying that it was a private course and he wouldn't be able to get in, but Melanie assured him that he would, and guess what, he did!

So, Harriet paid the cab driver, then she and Melanie got out of the cab and walked into the hotel. One of the men who was on duty at the desk said, "Well, we have some late night partiers!" Harriet and Melanie walked on up to the desk and Harriet told the desk clerk that they wanted to check into their room. The desk clerk told her that he had no vacancies and Harriet told him that they had reservations. The clerk insisted there were no rooms. At this point, Harriet pulled her phone out of her game day bag, with the charging cord attached, and slapped it up onto the transaction counter of the desk and opened the email from the agency with which she and Melanie (you remember it was a tag team affair) made the reservation. You guessed it, Cheap Hotels.com. was the source for their hotel reservation. Harriet pointed out that the confirmation email stated that the booking at the Hilton in Montebello was guaranteed. The young man at the desk insisted that he did not have a room, but they would probably be able to find a room nearby. Harriet told him that she had just paid a cab driver $40 to bring her to this hotel where she had been guaranteed that she had a room and she didn't intend to pay to go to another hotel. She suggested that he call the booking agency and take the matter up with them and he did. The young man had just realized that he was dealing with a woman who knew her rights and had dealt with far more challenging adversaries in her career than a mere hotel clerk. He knew he was beaten.

While he was talking to the person at the booking agency, Harriet was thinking that if the room situation could not be resolved, she would just go into the restroom in the lobby, change into her monkey sock print pajamas and go to sleep on one of the nice sofas in the hotel lobby. She didn't know until the next day that Melanie had already picked out the banquette seat in the far corner of the dining room as her bed for the night.

The young man at the desk indicated to Harriet that she should talk with the person from the booking agency. The conversation started out pleasantly enough, but then the woman at the other end of the line mentioned how sorry she was that Harriet had a problem. Harriet very quickly pointed out that SHE did not have a problem, that it was indeed the booking agency and/or the hotel with the problem. Harriet then told the person with the booking agency that she was going to give the phone back to the young man at the desk and they would need to come up with a solution for THEIR problem. The young man and the person on the other end of the line talked for a while and the man at the desk informed Harriet they had found a room for the pair at a Best Western. Harriet shook her head and said, "That's not going to cut it." The man resumed his conversation and in a few minutes stated they had found a room at the Doubletree nearby and Melanie said, "That will be fine."

So they were chauffeured by the young man who had been lingering in the office adjacent to the front desk at the Hilton to the Doubletree Hotel in Montebello or somewhere near there, it could have been Rosemeade, but no one knows for certain because they thought they had gone to Pasadena. As it turned out, the young man was the security guard. He was well-dressed, wearing a white collared shirt, tie and nice slacks. As he drove the two sisters to their hotel in his personal vehicle, he was very courteous and chatted about his recent move to California and how much he enjoyed the warm weather. He had moved there from the Northeast and was especially glad not to be at his former place of residence that night because his former hometown was getting blasted with snow and extremely cold temperatures. There was no snow in Alabama that night, but temperatures were in the single digits and in Sprott, the temperature was 6 degrees.

And so, the sisters, weary but content, finally arrived at their hotel. The desk clerk at the Doubletree was on high alert for them and had obviously been warned that this pair was to be handled gently. Melanie was reminded of one of her favorite Eagles melodies, *"Welcome to the Hotel California, Such a lovely place...Plenty of room at the Hotel California"*. . . . a room which had previously been so elusive during those early morning hours had finally become a reality. Two beds had never looked lovelier. They plugged in their dead phones, got ready for bed, and went to sleep. But, just before Harriet fell asleep, she thought about a saying that she heard from time to time back home. People often said, "If you're gonna be dumb, you gotta be tough." Although she didn't put Melanie and herself into the category of being dumb, she did think they were pretty tough. The time was now about 4:30 a.m. CST on Tuesday morning. She and Melanie had gotten up around 5:30 am. CST on Sunday morning and had not been back to bed since then. They had engineered a path around the cancellation of four flights and a reservation mishap at the hotel and had managed to make it to the game. And, they had a fabulous time all along the way. She smiled as she drifted off into a deep, peaceful slumber.

Harriet woke up the next day and the first thing she thought of was that she hadn't talked to Cleve since she was in the taxi the night before. So, she grabbed her phone and went into the bathroom where she could talk to him without waking up Melanie. Cleve was glad to know that they were still alive. He had told their neighbor, Charles Nichols that the last time he heard from Melanie and Harriet had been the night before when they were riding around in Los Angeles in a taxi cab and he wasn't sure exactly what happened to them after that, but he thought he would have heard by now if something bad had occurred. After talking to Cleve, Harriet called Courtney and Larkin and recounted the adventures that she and Melanie had after the last time they talked to each other during the taxi ride the evening before. She was sitting on the side of the tub while talking and realized that she was talking loud enough to wake up everyone in the hotel and was sure she had awakened Melanie by that time. As she walked out into the room, her worries about that were confirmed. Melanie was up and rummaging through her stuff and in the process of getting ready. So, they took baths, which were indeed a much enjoyed simple pleasure, and got dressed for the rest of their journey.

The night before as they had been chauffeured to the Doubletree by the security guard from the Hilton, Melanie and Harriet noticed a mall that was very close to the hotel where they ultimately landed. So, their goal was to set out to find it. As luck would have it, the mall was directly across the street from the front door of the hotel. So, off they went to see what they could find. In case you hadn't guessed, Melanie and Harriet enjoy shopping as much as they enjoy football. When they got across the street, they decided they would look for a place to eat and their eyes landed on an Olive Garden and they decided that would be a good place for lunch. The restaurant was not very busy that day and they were seated immediately. Their server was a very handsome young man. They later learned that his name was Adam Perez. Whether it was because he decided that if he chatted these two old birds up he would get a fat tip or that he was genuinely intrigued by them, he was very attentive and charming during lunch. Adam earned his tip because he was kept busy toting bourbon drinks to Melanie and toasted marshmallow martinis to Harriet.

Melanie and Harriet settled in and posted pictures and comments on Facebook. They were happy to be sharing the experience with their friends back in Alabama. Donna Huey was once again sharing a happy time with the two girls, even if it was from a great distance. They had been friends all of their lives and had shared many adventures. Barbara, Debra, Buffy, Lori, and many others had followed their journey via Facebook. Melanie's picture standing in front of the Rose Bowl was posted and then the picture of Melanie's thumb that was to have been a picture of Harriet standing in front of the Rose Bowl was also posted. During the meal, Harriet and Melanie learned that Adam knew next to nothing about football and had not been aware that the BCS Championship Game had been played in close proximity to the restaurant only the evening before. They tried to explain to him how much fun it was to attend a football game and Harriet finally told him that he just had to come to Auburn and attend a game with them. So, they made plans to do that and Adam gave Harriet his email address and they all promised that they would be in touch.

As they were about to leave the restaurant, Melanie decided that it was time to call the Super Shuttle to reserve a ride back to the airport that evening. The phone call was going well until the Super Shuttle reservations clerk needed a street address at which they were to be collected. Melanie and Harriet only knew that they were in an Olive Garden that was across the street from the Doubletree, but had no clue what the name of the town might be, much less what the physical address of the hotel might be. So, they had to solicit help from their friends at Olive Garden to help them tell the Super Shuttle staff where to pick them up that evening. While this was going on, an Olive Garden customer was on her way out the door and the lady stopped to ask Harriet about the tiger stripe shawl that she was wearing. The woman was very interested in the shawl and asked if Harriet had made it. So Harriet took the shawl off and showed the lady how the shawl had been constructed and they chatted about sewing and crafts for a while before the lady exited from the building. At that point, Melanie had concluded the arrangements with Super Shuttle and Adam and a friend emerged from around the corner. Adam heartily hugged them both and wished them well on their journey. And with that fond farewell, the two old girls wandered over to Macy's to spend the rest of the afternoon shopping.

They entered the store in the cosmetic department and immediately started looking for something to give to Courtney as a thank you gift for the bag filled with goodies she had given to them before they left Alabama on Sunday. The chocolate that was in the bag had been their mainstay for several days. And, they didn't really need an excuse to shop for Courtney because she was a fun person to shop for because she liked all of the same things they did; everything that was fun, fluffy, furry, flashy, faceted, flirty, flamboyant, feathery, fine, and otherwise fabulous was right up their alley. So, they found some gel nail polish kits that seemed to be the perfect thing to take home to Courtney. They wandered around the store and touched and felt everything in there and bought some socks because neither of them was pleased with the socks they were wearing. They then went out into the mall, sat down on a bench and proceeded to put on the new socks.

The afternoon had passed quickly and the sisters decided that they should find a place to eat supper because it would soon be time to meet the shuttle at the Doubletree and head back to the airport. They found a little restaurant inside the mall and had some more drinks and a light snack. Harriet noticed that every single person in the restaurant was wearing black. EVERYONE!! So, they looked like two vibrant peacocks in the midst of a flock of crows. What a wonderful situation in which to find themselves!

After leaving the restaurant they went back across the street to the Doubletree and the Super Shuttle soon arrived to whisk them back to the airport in Los Angeles. After arriving at the airport, they decided to sit in the ticketing area for a while before going through security. As they were sitting there, all of a sudden, Harriet realized that they would have to find a way to get the gel nail polish they had purchased for Courtney inside their zip lock bags in order to get it through security. So, she and Melanie fumbled and sorted and reorganized their little plastic bottles inside the bags and finally got everything stuffed inside. Then they made their way through security and into the boarding area.

As they were headed to their gate, they almost ran head-on into Paul Finebaum. The encounter caused Harriet to remember what Paul had said about the condition of the Rose Bowl on a radio show back in the fall. A Bama fan was making plans to attend the championship game and called to ask Paul about the championship game in 2009 when Alabama played there and they wanted to know more about the venue. The word that Paul used to describe the condition of the Rose Bowl was, "woeful". And even though Harriet didn't realize when she heard him say that how accurate the description was, she now knew exactly what he meant.

Going Home

They spent a while in the airport and had a conversation
with a very disgruntled Auburn fan from Atlanta. They
later decided he was just a disgruntled person in general,
because how could you possibly be disgruntled about
Auburn? Neither Harriet nor Melanie would allow him to
be negative about their Tigers and they told him how proud
they were of the team and the fabulous season they had.
And then the time came for them to board the plane. It was
12:35 a.m. on Wednesday when they departed LAX. They
were seated together in the back of the plane. As the plane
took off, they settled in, took off their shoes, and sharing
the tiger stripe shawl as a blanket, prepared for the long
flight to Charlotte. When they arrived in Charlotte that
morning, Harriet couldn't locate her shoes and the young
woman sitting next to Melanie couldn't find her phone.
Perhaps more went on during the flight than they
remembered, but eventually Harriet was able to drag her
boots from underneath the seat in front of her and the
person sitting behind the young lady found her phone. So,
with all of their stuff gathered up, Melanie and Harriet
deplaned and went into the terminal in Charlotte. They
didn't have long to wait between flights, so they quickly
scampered along the moving sidewalks in order to get to
their gate for the flight to Birmingham.

Along the way, they decided to get something for breakfast.
They stopped at a counter where country style breakfasts
were being dished out. They bought almost the same
things but Melanie's breakfast cost about $3 while Harriet
forked out $11 for her plate of grits, bacon, eggs, biscuit
and coffee, most of which wound up in the trashcan. The
gate from which they were leaving was a throwback to
another era in air travel. There was no jet way through
which they could walk to get to the airplane. Instead, they

had to walk outside, across the tarmac, and up the stairs into the plane. The morning was bright and sunny, but bitterly cold. There was a young lady standing near them waiting her turn to board the plane. Harriet wondered if the young woman's legs might freeze before she made it to the airplane because she had on a very short skirt and absolutely nothing on her legs.

While they were standing around waiting to board, Melanie and Harriet noticed that Jameis Winston's parents and little brother were waiting to board the plane also. So, they walked over to them and Melanie and Harriet congratulated them on the victory the night before and the awards that their son had received and the good game that he played on Monday night. Mr. Winston commented that it was not a good game until it was over because he thought they might lose until after the last second ticked off the clock. Harriet and Melanie reminded them that the game was really not so unusual from the perspective of heart-stopping finishes for Auburn fans and that most Auburn fans had already had pacemakers installed just to get them through the season with the Miracle Workers. Melanie mentioned that her grandson, Kevin attended FSU and was very happy about the results of the game. Mr. Winston asked her what his "classification" was and she told him that he was a freshman and that he was interested in a career in sports management. Mr. Winston said that Kevin needed to talk to Jameis and Harriet asked him if they could give him Kevin's number to give to Jameis so that Jameis could call Kevin. They somehow found a scrap of paper and Melanie gave Kevin's number to Jameis Winston's father and then they all boarded the plane.

Harriet and Melanie decided to celebrate the last leg of their flight by drinking Bloody Marys. They were on the very back seat of the plane and the flight attendant stood beside them and chatted during much of the trip, at least during the time when she wasn't reading the Bible. As they landed in Birmingham, Mr. Winston, who was sitting two rows in front of them, passed the phone back and told Melanie that Jameis wanted to talk to her. So, there they were, sitting in the plane in Birmingham, taxiing to the gate, and Melanie was talking on the phone to Jameis Winston, Heisman Trophy Winner, quarterback of the national champions, and possibly the most well-known student athlete in the universe. Traveling with Melanie and Harriet is kind of like travelling with Forrest Gump. They always have chocolate and they are always going to be in the middle of something exciting.

And so the journey ended. As they walked into the terminal in Birmingham, Jameis Winston's mother was standing just inside. Harriet stopped and hugged her and told her that she had been so worried about her. Jameis' mother asked, "Why?" Harriet told her that she was concerned because she had not known until earlier that morning whether she and Jameis' father and little brother had made all of their connections and made it to Los Angeles on Sunday. She told Mrs. Winston that she knew that it would have broken her heart if she had not made it to the Rose Bowl to see Jameis play. They hugged again and then Harriet and Melanie walked into the ticketing area and into the arms of Cleve, who gave them big hugs and kisses.

They were glad to have been where they had been and they were glad to be home again. Life would never be quite the same, because they learned something about themselves and about each other that they may not have known completely before the trip. Since the time that Harriet was born when Melanie was only 22 months old, their names have always been spoken together, as if they are one person. It has always been "Melanie and Harriet", never, just Melanie, never, just Harriet. They are the dynamic duo, the yin and the yang, peanut butter and jelly....two sisters with complimentary talents and a shared love of all things in life. Through the years, the two sisters have comforted each other through broken hearts, divorces, and the loss of loved ones, and they have celebrated births, graduations, marriages, birthdays, promotions, Auburn football and other important events. Soon they will celebrate retirement and then there will be more time for travel and visits with each other. More time together will undoubtedly equal more fun!

They enjoyed the trip to the BCS Championship Game that took them to Birmingham, Montgomery, Dallas, San Francisco, Los Angeles, Pasadena, Montebello, Rosemeade, and Charlotte...every second of it. They would have also enjoyed going to Las Vegas, Phoenix, and Tucson, but apparently that was not in the cards for this journey. The trip was a sweet victory and caused them to remember that it is possible to enjoy moments like these because "we work hard in the Sprang...and the Fall...and the Winter." They also realized that you can experience a profound sense of accomplishment if you are willing to put forth every ounce of effort that is required to accomplish your goal and fulfill your dream.
Ain't no easy way in life, Baby!

W a r E a g l e!
Beat Bama!

Credits and Acknowledgements

"The Little Old Lady from Pasadena" is a song written by Don Altfeld, Jan Berry and Roger Christian, and recorded by 1960s American pop singers, Jan and Dean Writing credits for the song, "Hotel California" are shared by Don Felder, Don Henley, and Glenn Frey.
"Hotel California" is a hit song that was sung by the Eagles. Writing credits for the song are shared by Don Felder, Don Henley, and Glenn Frey.
"California Dreamin'" is a song by The Mamas & the Papas, first released in 1965. The lyrics of the song express the narrator's longing for the warmth of California during a cold winter. It was written by John and Michelle Phillips.

The names of the characters in this story have not been changed to protect the innocent. We want to give credit to all of the people mentioned because they have influenced our lives and they are all loved. This is also to acknowledge that we would like to have an opportunity to see the Auburn fans that we sat beside in the Rose Bowl again and get to know them better. Our brief encounter with them did not give us enough time to appreciate them for the wonderful human beings that they undoubtedly are.

And once again, thanks, Pat Dye. No one can say, "Ain't no easy way in life" in quite the same way that you can.

Respectful Request for Refund

From: Melanie Harrison
To: "refunds@usairways.com" <refunds@usairways.com>
Sent: Tuesday, January 21, 2014 1:07 PM
Subject: Refund request on D4TTY5

I spoke with Jason in your refund dept. 1/20/14 regarding a request to refund cancelled flights on itinerary D4TTY5 on January 5 and 6 , 2014 and AA 2819 flight from MGM to DFW on Jan. 6 for Melanie Oakes Harrison and Harriet Oakes Deason. You should have his documentation on file. Jason asked that I send you an email to complete my request.

On Jan. 5, 2014, our USAir flight from BHM to CLT was cancelled and we were deplaned in BHM and told to find other flights to get to our final destination of LA and the BCS Championship game on Jan. 6. Our original destination was Las Vegas, but USAir nor American could get us to Las Vegas in time to catch our charter bus from Las Vegas to LA to the game so we began efforts to get to LA or surrounding area. An amazing USAir clerk in BHM, Marie, and her supervisor, Don, worked for over 3 hours to find us flights to get us from BHM to BUR for which we were very grateful via

AA1271 BHMDFW
AA1055 DFWTUS
US2883 TUSPHX
US2848 PHXBUR

At approx. 1:30 a.m. on Jan. 6 I received notice the AA1271 flight out of BHM had been cancelled. I attempted to call USAir and American to check on other options but was put on hold with estimated wait time of 2 hours. Using our smartphones, we found a flight AA2819 from MGM to DFW which would allow us to make our other flights. BHM is 110 miles from MGM. We could not wait for an agent and had to make a quick decision to purchase this flight as my brother-in-law had to drive 1 1/2

69

hours back to BHM to pick us up and then drive another 2 hours to get us to MGM. I was charged $361 per person on reservation RLBHLK which I booked through American website. Sometime before 2:30 a.m. Jan 6 I spoke with a USAir rep who also booked me on the AA2819 flight as part of D4TTY5 and said I would not be charged for RLBHLK. However, my credit card was charged for 2 seats on AA2819. We got to MGM and made flight AA2819 to DFW. When we arrived in DFW, we learned flights AA1055 and US 2883 were cancelled. I spoke with another USAir agent on the phone who could not get us to LA in time for the BCS game nor get us back to BHM that day. I spoke with another USAir agent on the phone approx. 30 minutes later to be sure our flights from LAX to BHM through CLT on Jan. 8 were still valid on D4TTY5 which she said they were and that she was declaring the flights from DFW, TUS, PHX and BUR to be of no value. We did find a Virgin American flight that took us from DFW to SFO to LAX and we got to the BCS game a while after it had started.

The only flights that we actually used on reservation D4TTY5 were US492 LAXCLT and US4727 CLTBHM on Jan 8. I respectfully request refunds for all other flights on this itinerary. It would also be nice if you could pay for the Virgin American tickets Flights VX 936 and VX 715on Jan 6 which totaled $986.72 and which actually got us to our destination.

I want to say that all USAir agents with whom we spoke were very friendly and tried to be helpful. Please advise if you need any further information from me.

Sincerely,

Melanie Oakes Harrison

A Special Anniversary

50 years ago today Melanie and I made our first trip to Cliff Hare Stadium. President Kennedy had been murdered the day before. My school teacher, Ruth Oakes, cried that Friday as she told us that our President had been killed in Dallas. School was dismissed, the whole world was in turmoil, and Melanie and I were worried that the Auburn-Florida State game scheduled for the next day would be cancelled. But, thankfully, it was not.

So many memories come flooding back as I think of all the games during the past 50 years....fried chicken, pineapple sandwiches, pound cakes, my Mamma's and Mamma Miller's cashmere coats, fur pillbox hats, and lizard and alligator high heel shoes that they wore to the games, my cousin John McAfee looking up from a group of friends and with a huge grin on his face yelling across the parlor in Sewell Hall--"Here come them purdy girls from Sprott" a memory that still almost brings tears to my eyes every time I think about it. We met our rock stars that day--Bill Cody, Jimmy Sidle, Tucker Frederickson, Woody Woodall, and all of the Auburn team. What a dream come true!

I attended Auburn football games as a little girl, a tween, a teenager, a young wife, a young mother, an old wife, an old mother, the mother of a player and now as a grandmother. My sister, Melanie, has always been there too. What precious memories we share of these past 50 years. I remember Melanie and I going to a game with our children, my husband, Mama, Daddy, and my grandmother, Mama Miller. My son, Larkin was the youngest of our three children. He was 2 at the time. The children were dressed in matching Auburn outfits and were excited about the trip.

As we made our way up the spiral to the new upper deck on the West side of the stadium on a scorching hot day, Mama Miller and Daddy stopped frequently to smoke a cigarette. The upper deck had just been completed and was open that game day for the very first time. There were a few kinks that had not been worked out prior to the inaugural event. The temperature hovered at 100 degrees and the concession stands in the upper deck ran out of ice, water, and Cokes. I seem to remember some issues with the restrooms but have thankfully forgotten all of the details about that. We sat with our small children on the front row of the upper deck with only a thin rail between us and the seats far below us and kept their arms tightly clutched in our hands to prevent them from falling to a certain death. We were all hot, Tennessee took us to the wood shed and gave us a sound beating, but, it was still a good day, because we were at Auburn.

One of the greatest thrills in my life was to watch my son run out of the tunnel in an Auburn football uniform. I always got to the stadium early just to be able to see him warm up. There have been great days at Jordan-Hare. The victory over Alabama in 1997 was huge. The fake field goal in 2000 against Vanderbilt, when #63 was on the field for a touchdown. The 2010 season was magical. Last week against Georgia was phenomenal!

I look forward to many more good times at Auburn. And when my life here on earth has been completed, I hope that you may run into me at Jordan-Hare sometime. I will be sitting on the brick wall around the flower bed in the southwest corner of the stadium....see you there, forever.

Written by, Harriet Oakes Deason
November 23, 2013

The Bag

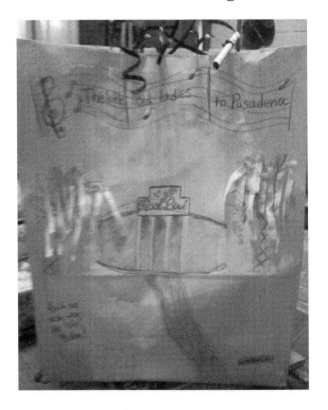

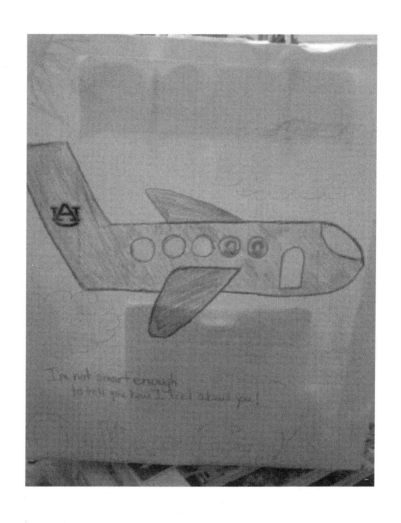

74

The Texts

Test message from Larkin:
Larkin- January 5, 9:08 pm:
Hey, mom. Just checking to see if you guys had made it yet. I love you! I am SOOOOO happy you two are on this mission! WAR EAGLE! D.B.A.D.

Harriet-January 5, 9:29 pm:
Our flight to Charlotte cancelled. Still in Birmingham trying to get a flight out.

Larkin-January 5, 9:31 pm:
OMG! I am soooo sorry! Let me know.

Harriet-January 5, 9:31 pm:
OK

Harriet-January5, 9:48 pm:
Got it!!!!! We will leave tomorrow morning.

Larkin-January 5, 9:53 pm
Holy cow! Well you were right about staying up tonight. Where is the liquor? When did you find out you were cancelled?

Harriet-January 6, 2:37 am:
Our flight cancelled out of Birmingham. Leaving Montgomery at 7 to make connection to Dallas.

Larkin-January 6, 9:58 am:
Are you close to at least seeing some planes? Montgomery?!!??!!!??

Harriet-January 6, 12:09 pm:

In Dallas. Waiting to leave at 1:45 for LA. When we arrived our flights had been cancelled. Had to scramble once again and rebook. WAR DAMN EAGLE!!!

Larkin-January 6, 12:16 pm:
That is cutting it close, sister!

Larkin-January 6, 1:08 pm:
What a story!

Larkin-January 6, 6:02 pm:
Are you in the air? I really hope I don't hear back in a while…FOR YOUR SAKE!

Larkin-January 6, 6:02 pm:
Almost there just boarded for a short flight to LA from San Fran I think we are going to make it for more than half the game
Larkin-January 6, 7:40 pm:
Omg! Just in time! I love you.

Larkin-January 6, 7:40 pm:
Just took the field. Where the _____ are u!

Larkin-January 6, 7:58 pm:
Clark just landed a punt (not downed by someone) on the 3!

Larkin-January 6, 8:00 pm:
3&out!!!!!!!!!!!!!!!!! Go D!

Larkin-January 6, 8:22 pm:
Td and pat. 7-3 Auburn!

Harriet-January 6, 8:23 pm:
That's what I'm talking about

Larkin-January 6, 8:24 pm:
YES! RUTHERENOW

Harriet-January 6, 8:25 pm:
We are in rush hour traffic probably another 20 min

Harriet-January 6, 9:26 pm:
Were here

Larkin-January 6, 10:11 pm:
Thank God. I'm going to bed now.

Larkin-January 6, 10:12 pm:
Have ya met, Dee Ford!?

Harriet to Courtney-January 6, 4:54 am:
Daddy drove us to Montgomery and is on his way back to Birmingham, Please tx him when you get up

Courtney-January 6, 6:02 pm:
How's it going?

Courtney-January 6, 6:02pm:
Fight on you Orange and Blue! (with photo of Rose Bowl)

Harriet-January 6, 6:03 pm:
Almost there just boarded flight yup LA

Harriet-January 6, 6:03 pm
Go go go !!!

Courtney-January 6, 7:40 pm:
Do it!

Courtney-January 6, 7:40 pm:

Are u there yet?

Courtney-January 6, 8:27 pm:
We're Winning!

Harriet-January 6, 8:27 pm:
I kno keep up the good work were hooked Em to the ground

Courtney-January 6, 8:29 pm:
You're there?

Harriet-January 6, 8:29 pm:
Not. Y et but making hoops progress.

Courtney-January 6, 9:22 pm:
Are you there yet?

Harriet-January 6, 9:26 pm:
Were here

Courtney-January 6, 10:11 pm:
Hallelujah   Prove it!

Courtney-January 7, 12:43 am:
Did y'all get a place to stay?

Harriet-January 7, 3:50 am:
Well yes but that is another story

Courtney-January 8, 9:43 am:
If this is Wednesday, this is Birmingham.

From Renee to Harriet
January 6, 8:00 pm:

Hey Hariette! It's Renee, I really need u at that stadium.
War Damn Eagle! Love from Greensboro.

Harriet-January 6, 8:34 pm:
Be there soon baby hold on.
Renee-January 6, 8:34 pm:
You go girl!!

Renee-January 6, 10:11 pm:
Get in that stadium they need u!!!

The Game

The Tickets

Made in the USA
Charleston, SC
27 August 2014